SNOW-BOUND AT EAGLE'S

BRET HARTE

1st WORLD
LIBRARY
Literary Society

Snow-Bound at Eagle's

Bret Harte

© 1st World Library, 2007
PO Box 2211
Fairfield, IA 52556
www.1stworldlibrary.com
First Edition

LCCN: 2007934095

Softcover ISBN: 978-1-4218-9626-7
Hardcover ISBN: 978-1-4218-9726-4
eBook ISBN: 978-1-4218-9526-0

Purchase *"Snow-Bound at Eagle's"*
as a traditional bound book at:
www.1stWorldLibrary.com/purchase.asp?ISBN=978-1-4218-9626-7

1st World Library is a literary, educational organization
dedicated to:

- Creating a free internet library of downloadable ebooks

- Hosting writing competitions and offering book publishing
scholarships.

Interested in more 1st World Library books? contact:
literacy@1stworldlibrary.com
Check us out at: www.1stworldlibrary.com

1ˢᵗ World Library Literary Society

Giving Back to the World

"If you want to work on the core problem, it's early school literacy."

- James Barksdale, former CEO of Netscape

"No skill is more crucial to the future of a child, or to a democratic and prosperous society, than literacy."

- Los Angeles Times

"Literacy... means far more than learning how to read and write... The aim is to transmit... knowledge and promote social participation."

- UNESCO

"Literacy is not a luxury, it is a right and a responsibility. If our world is to meet the challenges of the twenty-first century we must harness the energy and creativity of all our citizens."

- President Bill Clinton

"Parents should be encouraged to read to their children, and teachers should be equipped with all available techniques for teaching literacy, so the varying needs and capacities of individual kids can be taken into account."

- Hugh Mackay

CHAPTER I

For some moments profound silence and darkness had accompanied a Sierran stage-coach towards the summit. The huge, dim bulk of the vehicle, swaying noiselessly on its straps, glided onward and upward as if obeying some mysterious impulse from behind, so faint and indefinite appeared its relation to the viewless and silent horses ahead. The shadowy trunks of tall trees that seemed to approach the coach windows, look in, and then move hurriedly away, were the only distinguishable objects. Yet even these were so vague and unreal that they might have been the mere phantoms of some dream of the half-sleeping passengers; for the thickly-strewn needles of the pine, that choked the way and deadened all sound, yielded under the silently-crushing wheels a faint soporific odor that seemed to benumb their senses, already slipping back into unconsciousness during the long ascent. Suddenly the stage stopped.

Three of the four passengers inside struggled at once into upright wakefulness. The fourth passenger, John Hale, had not been sleeping, and turned impatiently towards the window. It seemed to him that two of the moving trees had suddenly become motionless outside. One of them moved again, and the door opened quickly but quietly, as of itself.

"Git down," said a voice in the darkness.

All the passengers except Hale started. The man next to him moved his right hand suddenly behind him, but as quickly stopped. One of the motionless trees had apparently closed upon the vehicle, and what had seemed to be a bough projecting from it at right angles changed slowly into the faintly shining double-barrels of a gun at the window.

"Drop that!" said the voice.

The man who had moved uttered a short laugh, and returned his hand empty to his knees. The two others perceptibly shrugged their shoulders as over a game that was lost. The remaining passenger, John Hale, fearless by nature, inexperienced by habit, awaking suddenly to the truth, conceived desperate resistance. But without his making a gesture this was instinctively felt by the others; the muzzle of the gun turned spontaneously on him, and he was vaguely conscious of a certain contempt and impatience of him in his companions.

"Git down," repeated the voice imperatively.

The three passengers descended. Hale, furious, alert, but helpless of any opportunity, followed. He was surprised to find the stage-driver and express messenger standing beside him; he had not heard them dismount. He instinctively looked towards the horses. He could see nothing.

"Hold up your hands!"

One of the passengers had already lifted his, in a weary, perfunctory way. The others did the same reluctantly and awkwardly, but apparently more from the consciousness of the ludicrousness of their attitude than from any sense of danger. The rays of a bull's-eye lantern, deftly managed by invisible hands, while it left the intruders in shadow,

Bret Harte

completely illuminated the faces and figures of the passengers. In spite of the majestic obscurity and silence of surrounding nature, the group of humanity thus illuminated was more farcical than dramatic. A scrap of newspaper, part of a sandwich, and an orange peel that had fallen from the floor of the coach, brought into equal prominence by the searching light, completed the absurdity.

"There's a man here with a package of greenbacks," said the voice, with an official coolness that lent a certain suggestion of Custom House inspection to the transaction; "who is it?" The passengers looked at each other, and their glance finally settled on Hale.

"It's not HIM," continued the voice, with a slight tinge of contempt on the emphasis. "You'll save time and searching, gentlemen, if you'll tote it out. If we've got to go through every one of you we'll try to make it pay."

The significant threat was not unheeded. The passenger who had first moved when the stage stopped put his hand to his breast.

"T'other pocket first, if you please," said the voice.

The man laughed, drew a pistol from his hip pocket, and, under the strong light of the lantern, laid it on a spot in the road indicated by the voice. A thick envelope, taken from his breast pocket, was laid beside it. "I told the d—d fools that gave it to me, instead of sending it by express, it would be at their own risk," he said apologetically.

"As it's going with the express now it's all the same," said the inevitable humorist of the occasion, pointing to the despoiled express treasure-box already in the road.

The intention and deliberation of the outrage was plain enough to Hale's inexperience now. Yet he could not understand the cool acquiescence of his fellow-passengers, and was furious. His reflections were interrupted by a voice which seemed to come from a greater distance. He fancied it was even softer in tone, as if a certain austerity was relaxed.

"Step in as quick as you like, gentlemen. You've five minutes to wait, Bill."

The passengers reentered the coach; the driver and express messenger hurriedly climbed to their places. Hale would have spoken, but an impatient gesture from his companions stopped him. They were evidently listening for something; he listened too.

Yet the silence remained unbroken. It seemed incredible that there should be no indication near or far of that forceful presence which a moment ago had been so dominant. No rustle in the wayside "brush," nor echo from the rocky canyon below, betrayed a sound of their flight. A faint breeze stirred the tall tips of the pines, a cone dropped on the stage roof, one of the invisible horses that seemed to be listening too moved slightly in his harness. But this only appeared to accentuate the profound stillness. The moments were growing interminable, when the voice, so near as to startle Hale, broke once more from the surrounding obscurity.

"Good-night!"

It was the signal that they were free. The driver's whip cracked like a pistol shot, the horses sprang furiously forward, the huge vehicle lurched ahead, and then bounded violently after them. When Hale could make his voice heard in the confusion—a confusion which seemed greater from the colorless intensity of their last few moments' experience —he said hurriedly, "Then that fellow was there all the time?"

"I reckon," returned his companion, "he stopped five minutes to cover the driver with his double-barrel, until the two other men got off with the treasure."

"The TWO others!" gasped Hale. "Then there were only THREE men, and we SIX."

The man shrugged his shoulders. The passenger who had given up the greenbacks drawled, with a slow, irritating tolerance, "I reckon you're a stranger here?"

"I am—to this sort of thing, certainly, though I live a dozen miles from here, at Eagle's Court," returned Hale scornfully.

"Then you're the chap that's doin' that fancy ranchin' over at Eagle's," continued the man lazily.

"Whatever I'm doing at Eagle's Court, I'm not ashamed of it," said Hale tartly; "and that's more than I can say of what I've done—or HAVEN'T done—to-night. I've been one of six men over-awed and robbed by THREE."

"As to the over-awin', ez you call it—mebbee you know more about it than us. As to the robbin'—ez far as I kin remember, YOU haven't onloaded much. Ef you're talkin' about what OUGHTER have been done, I'll tell you what COULD have happened. P'r'aps ye noticed that when he pulled up I made a kind of grab for my wepping behind me?"

"I did; and you wern't quick enough," said Hale shortly.

"I wasn't quick enough, and that saved YOU. For ef I got that pistol out and in sight o' that man that held the gun—"

"Well," said Hale impatiently, "he'd have hesitated."

"He'd hev blown YOU with both barrels outer the window, and that before I'd got a half-cock on my revolver."

"But that would have been only one man gone, and there would have been five of you left," said Hale haughtily.

"That might have been, ef you'd contracted to take the hull charge of two handfuls of buck-shot and slugs; but ez one eighth o' that amount would have done your business, and yet left enough to have gone round, promiskiss, and satisfied the other passengers, it wouldn't do to kalkilate upon."

"But the express messenger and the driver were armed," continued Hale.

"They were armed, but not FIXED; that makes all the difference."

"I don't understand."

"I reckon you know what a duel is?"

"Yes."

"Well, the chances agin US was about the same as you'd have ef you was put up agin another chap who was allowed to draw a bead on you, and the signal to fire was YOUR DRAWIN' YOUR WEAPON. You may be a stranger to this sort o' thing, and p'r'aps you never fought a duel, but even then you wouldn't go foolin' your life away on any such chances."

Something in the man's manner, as in a certain sly amusement the other passengers appeared to extract from the conversation, impressed Hale, already beginning to be conscious of the ludicrous insufficiency of his own grievance beside that of his interlocutor.

"Then you mean to say this thing is inevitable," said he bitterly, but less aggressively.

"Ez long ez they hunt YOU; when you hunt THEM you've got the advantage, allus provided you know how to get at them ez well as they know how to get at you. This yer coach is bound to go regular, and on certain days. THEY ain't. By the time the sheriff gets out his posse they've skedaddled, and the leader, like as not, is takin' his quiet cocktail at the Bank Exchange, or mebbe losin' his earnings to the sheriff over draw poker, in Sacramento. You see you can't prove anything agin them unless you take them 'on the fly.' It may be a part of Joaquim Murietta's band, though I wouldn't swear to it."

"The leader might have been Gentleman George, from up-country," interposed a passenger. "He seemed to throw in a few fancy touches, particlerly in that 'Good night.' Sorter chucked a little sentiment in it. Didn't seem to be the same thing ez, 'Git, yer d—d suckers,' on the other line."

"Whoever he was, he knew the road and the men who travelled on it. Like ez not, he went over the line beside the driver on the box on the down trip, and took stock of everything. He even knew I had those greenbacks; though they were handed to me in the bank at Sacramento. He must have been hanging 'round there."

For some moments Hale remained silent. He was a civic-bred man, with an intense love of law and order; the kind of man who is the first to take that law and order into his own hands when he does not find it existing to please him. He had a Bostonian's respect for respectability, tradition, and propriety, but was willing to face irregularity and impropriety to create order elsewhere. He was fond of Nature with these limitations, never quite trusting her unguided instincts, and finding her as an instructress greatly inferior to Harvard University, though possibly not to Cornell. With dauntless enterprise and energy he had built and stocked a charming cottage farm in a nook in the Sierras, whence he opposed, like the lesser Englishman that he was, his own tastes to those of the alien West. In the present instance he felt it incumbent upon him not only to assert his principles, but to act upon them with his usual energy. How far he was impelled by the half-contemptuous passiveness of his companions it would be difficult to say.

"What is to prevent the pursuit of them at once?" he asked suddenly. "We are a few miles from the station, where horses can be procured."

"Who's to do it?" replied the other lazily. "The stage company will lodge the complaint with the authorities, but it will take two days to get the county officers out, and it's nobody else's funeral."

"I will go for one," said Hale quietly. "I have a horse waiting for me at the station, and can start at once."

There was an instant of silence. The stage-coach had left the obscurity of the forest, and by the stronger light Hale could perceive that his companion was examining him with two colorless, lazy eyes. Presently he said, meeting Hale's clear glance, but rather as if yielding to a careless reflection,—

"It MIGHT be done with four men. We oughter raise one

man at the station." He paused. "I don't know ez I'd mind taking a hand myself," he added, stretching out his legs with a slight yawn.

"Ye can count ME in, if you're goin', Kernel. I reckon I'm talkin' to Kernel Clinch," said the passenger beside Hale with sudden alacrity. "I'm Rawlins, of Frisco. Heerd of ye afore, Kernel, and kinder spotted you jist now from your talk."

To Hale's surprise the two men, after awkwardly and per-functorily grasping each other's hand, entered at once into a languid conversation on the recent election at Fresno, without the slightest further reference to the pursuit of the robbers. It was not until the remaining and undenominated passenger turned to Hale, and, regretting that he had immediate business at the Summit, offered to accompany the party if they would wait a couple of hours, that Colonel Clinch briefly returned to the subject.

"FOUR men will do, and ez we'll hev to take horses from the station we'll hev to take the fourth man from there."

With these words he resumed his uninteresting conversation with the equally uninterested Rawlins, and the undeno-minated passenger subsided into an admiring and dreamy contemplation of them both. With all his principle and really high-minded purpose, Hale could not help feeling cons-trained and annoyed at the sudden subordinate and auxiliary position to which he, the projector of the enterprise, had been reduced. It was true that he had never offered himself as their leader; it was true that the principle he wished to uphold and the effect he sought to obtain would be equally demonstrated under another; it was true that the execution of his own conception gravitated by some occult impulse to the man who had not sought it, and whom he had always regarded as an incapable. But all this was so unlike precedent or tradition that, after the fashion of conservative men, he was suspicious of it, and only that his honor was now involved he would have withdrawn from the enterprise. There was still a chance of reasserting himself at the station, where he was known, and where some authority might be deputed to him.

But even this prospect failed. The station, half hotel and half stable, contained only the landlord, who was also express agent, and the new volunteer who Clinch had suggested would be found among the stable-men. The nearest justice of the peace was ten miles away, and Hale had to abandon even his hope of being sworn in as a deputy constable. This introduction of a common and illiterate ostler into the party on equal terms with himself did not add to his satisfaction, and a remark from Rawlins seemed to complete his embarrassment.

"Ye had a mighty narrer escape down there just now," said that gentleman confidentially, as Hale buckled his saddle girths.

"I thought, as we were not supposed to defend ourselves, there was no danger," said Hale scornfully.

"Oh, I don't mean them road agents. But HIM."

"Who?"

"Kernel Clinch. You jist ez good as allowed he hadn't any grit."

"Whatever I said, I suppose I am responsible for it," answered Hale haughtily.

"That's what gits me," was the imperturbable reply. "He's the best shot in Southern California, and hez let daylight through a dozen chaps afore now for half what you said."

"Indeed!"

"Howsummever," continued Rawlins philosophically, "ez he's concluded to go WITH ye instead of FOR ye, you're likely to hev your ideas on this matter carried out up to the handle. He'll make short work of it, you bet. Ef, ez I suspect, the leader is an airy young feller from Frisco, who hez took to the road lately, Clinch hez got a personal grudge agin him from a quarrel over draw poker."

This was the last blow to Hale's ideal crusade. Here he was—an honest, respectable citizen—engaged as simple accessory to a lawless vendetta originating at a gambling table! When the first shock was over that grim philosophy which is the reaction of all imaginative and sensitive natures came to his aid. He felt better; oddly enough he began to be conscious that he was thinking and acting like his companions. With this feeling a vague sympathy, before absent, faintly showed itself in their actions. The Sharpe's rifle put into his hands by the stable-man was accompanied by a familiar word of suggestion as to an equal, which he was ashamed to find flattered him. He was able to continue the conversation with Rawlins more coolly.

"Then you suspect who is the leader?"

"Only on giniral principles. There was a finer touch, so to speak, in this yer robbery that wasn't in the old-fashioned style. Down in my country they hed crude ideas about them things—used to strip the passengers of everything, includin' their clothes. They say that at the station hotels, when the coach came in, the folks used to stand round with blankets to wrap up the passengers so ez not to skeer the wimen. Thar's a story that the driver and express manager drove up one day with only a copy of the Alty Californy wrapped around 'em; but thin," added Rawlins grimly, "there WAS folks ez said the hull story was only an advertisement got up for the Alty."

"Time's up."

"Are you ready, gentlemen?" said Colonel Clinch.

Hale started. He had forgotten his wife and family at Eagle's Court, ten miles away. They would be alarmed at his absence, would perhaps hear some exaggerated version of the stage coach robbery, and fear the worst.

"Is there any way I could send a line to Eagle's Court before daybreak?" he asked eagerly.

The station was already drained of its spare men and horses. The undenominated passenger stepped forward and offered to take it himself when his business, which he would despatch as quickly as possible, was concluded.

"That ain't a bad idea," said Clinch reflectively, "for ef yer hurry you'll head 'em off in case they scent us, and try to double back on the North Ridge. They'll fight shy of the trail if they see anybody on it, and one man's as good as a dozen."

Hale could not help thinking that he might have been that one man, and had his opportunity for independent action but for his rash proposal, but it was too late to withdraw now. He hastily scribbled a few lines to his wife on a sheet of the station paper, handed it to the man, and took his place in the little cavalcade as it filed silently down the road.

They had ridden in silence for nearly an hour, and had passed the scene of the robbery by a higher track. Morning had long ago advanced its colors on the cold white peaks to their right, and was taking possession of the spur where they rode.

"It looks like snow," said Rawlins quietly.

Hale turned towards him in astonishment. Nothing on earth or sky looked less likely. It had been cold, but that might have been only a current from the frozen peaks beyond, reaching the lower valley. The ridge on which they had halted was still thick with yellowish-green summer foliage, mingled with the darker evergreen of pine and fir. Oven-like canyons in the long flanks of the mountain seemed still to glow with the heat of yesterday's noon; the breathless air yet trembled and quivered over stifling gorges and passes in the granite rocks, while far at their feet sixty miles of perpetual summer stretched away over the winding American River, now and then lost in a gossamer haze. It was scarcely ripe October where they stood; they could see the plenitude of August still lingering in the valleys.

"I've seen Thomson's Pass choked up with fifteen feet o' snow earlier than this," said Rawlins, answering Hale's gaze; "and last September the passengers sledded over the road we came last night, and all the time Thomson, a mile lower down over the ridge in the hollow, smoking his pipes under roses in his piazzy! Mountains is mighty uncertain; they make their own weather ez they want it. I reckon you ain't wintered here yet."

Hale was obliged to admit that he had only taken Eagle's Court in the early spring.

"Oh, you're all right at Eagle's—when you're there! But it's like Thomson's—it's the gettin' there that—Hallo! What's that?"

A shot, distant but distinct, had rung through the keen air. It was followed by another so alike as to seem an echo.

"That's over yon, on the North Ridge," said the ostler, "about two miles as the crow flies and five by the trail. Somebody's shootin' b'ar."

"Not with a shot gun," said Clinch, quickly wheeling his horse with a gesture that electrified them. "It's THEM, and the've doubled on us! To the North Ridge, gentlemen, and ride all you know!"

It needed no second challenge to completely transform that quiet cavalcade. The wild man-hunting instinct, inseparable to most humanity, rose at their leader's look and word. With an incoherent and unintelligible cry, giving voice to the chase like the commonest hound of their fields, the order-loving Hale and the philosophical Rawlins wheeled with the others, and in another instant the little band swept out of sight in the forest.

An immense and immeasurable quiet succeeded. The sunlight glistened silently on cliff and scar, the vast distance below seemed to stretch out and broaden into repose. It might have been fancy, but over the sharp line of the North Ridge a light smoke lifted as of an escaping soul.

Bret Harte

CHAPTER II

Eagle's Court, one of the highest canyons of the Sierras, was in reality a plateau of table-land, embayed like a green lake in a semi-circular sweep of granite, that, lifting itself three thousand feet higher, became a foundation for the eternal snows. The mountain genii of space and atmosphere jealously guarded its seclusion and surrounded it with illusions; it never looked to be exactly what it was: the traveller who saw it from the North Ridge apparently at his feet in descending found himself separated from it by a mile-long abyss and a rushing river; those who sought it by a seeming direct trail at the end of an hour lost sight of it completely, or, abandoning the quest and retracing their steps, suddenly came upon the gap through which it was entered. That which from the Ridge appeared to be a copse of bushes beside the tiny dwelling were trees three hundred feet high; the cultivated lawn before it, which might have been covered by the traveller's handkerchief, was a field of a thousand acres.

The house itself was a long, low, irregular structure, chiefly of roof and veranda, picturesquely upheld by rustic pillars of pine, with the bark still adhering, and covered with vines and trailing roses. Yet it was evident that the coolness produced by this vast extent of cover was more than the architect, who had planned it under the influence of a staring and bewildering sky, had trustfully conceived, for it had to be mitigated by blazing fires in open hearths when the thermometer marked a hundred degrees in the field beyond. The dry, restless wind that continually rocked the tall masts of the pines with a sound like the distant sea, while it stimulated out-door physical exertion and defied fatigue, left the sedentary dwellers in these altitudes chilled in the shade they courted, or scorched them with heat when they ventured to bask supinely in the sun. White muslin curtains at the French windows, and rugs, skins, and heavy furs dispersed in the interior, with certain other charming but incongruous details of furniture, marked the inconsistencies of the climate.

There was a coquettish indication of this in the costume of Miss Kate Scott as she stepped out on the veranda that morning. A man's broad-brimmed Panama hat, partly unsexed by a twisted gayly-colored scarf, but retaining enough character to give piquancy to the pretty curves of the face beneath, protected her from the sun; a red flannel shirt—another spoil from the enemy—and a thick jacket shielded her from the austerities of the morning breeze. But the next inconsistency was peculiarly her own. Miss Kate always wore the freshest and lightest of white cambric skirts, without the least reference to the temperature. To the practical sanatory remonstrances of her brother-in-law, and to the conventional criticism of her sister, she opposed the same defence: "How else is one to tell when it is summer in this ridiculous climate? And then, woollen is stuffy, color draws the sun, and one at least knows when one is clean or dirty." Artistically the result was far from unsatisfactory. It was a pretty figure under the sombre pines, against the gray granite and the steely sky, and seemed to lend the yellowing fields from which the flowers had already fled a floral relief of color. I do not think the few masculine wayfarers of that locality objected to it; indeed, some had betrayed an indiscreet admiration, and had curiously followed the invitation of Miss Kate's warmly-colored figure until they had encountered the invincible indifference of Miss Kate's cold gray eyes. With these manifestations her brother-in-law did not concern himself; he had perfect confidence in her unqualified disinterest in the neighboring humanity, and permitted her to wander in her solitary picturesqueness, or accompanied her when she rode in her dark green habit, with equal freedom from anxiety.

For Miss Scott, although only twenty, had already subjected most of her maidenly illusions to mature critical analyses. She had voluntarily accompanied her sister and mother to California, in the earnest hope that nature contained something worth saying to her, and was disappointed to find she had already discounted its value in the pages of books. She hoped to find a vague freedom in this unconventional life thus opened to her, or rather to show others that she knew how intelligently to appreciate it, but as yet she was only able to express it in the one detail of dress already alluded to. Some of the men, and nearly all the women, she had met thus far, she was amazed to find, valued the conventionalities she believed she despised, and were voluntarily assuming the chains she thought she had thrown off. Instead of learning anything from them, these children of nature had bored her with eager questionings regarding the civilization she had abandoned, or irritated her with crude imitations of it for her benefit. "Fancy," she had written to a friend in Boston, "my calling on Sue Murphy, who remembered the Donner tragedy, and who once shot a grizzly that was prowling round her cabin, and think of her begging me to lend her my sack for a pattern, and wanting to know if 'polonays' were still worn." She remembered more bitterly the romance that had tickled her earlier fancy, told of two college friends of her brother-in-law's who were living the "perfect life" in the mines, laboring in the ditches with a copy of Homer in their pockets, and writing letters of the purest philosophy under the free air of the pines. How, coming unexpectedly on them in their Arcadia, the party found them unpresentable through dirt, and thenceforth unknowable through domestic complications that had filled their Arcadian cabin with half-breed children.

Much of this disillusion she had kept within her own heart, from a feeling of pride, or only lightly touched upon it in her relations with her mother and sister. For Mrs. Hale and Mrs. Scott had no idols to shatter, no enthusiasm to subdue. Firmly and unalterably conscious of their own superiority to the life they led and the community that surrounded them, they accepted their duties cheerfully, and performed them conscientiously. Those duties were loyalty to Hale's interests and a vague missionary work among the neighbors, which, like most missionary work, consisted rather in making their own ideas understood than in understanding the ideas of their audience. Old Mrs. Scott's zeal was partly religious, an inheritance from her Puritan ancestry; Mrs. Hale's was the affability of a gentlewoman and the obligation of her position. To this was added the slight languor of the cultivated American wife, whose health has been affected by the birth of her first child, and whose views of marriage and maternity were slightly tinged with gentle scepticism. She was sincerely attached to her husband, "who dominated the household" like the rest of his "women folk," with the faint consciousness of that division of service which renders the position of the sultan of a seraglio at once so prominent and so precarious. The attitude of John Hale in his family circle was dominant because it had never been subjected to criticism or comparison; and perilous for the same reason.

Mrs. Hale presently joined her sister in the veranda, and, shading her eyes with a narrow white hand, glanced on the prospect with a polite interest and ladylike urbanity. The searching sun, which, as Miss Kate once intimated, was "vulgarity itself," stared at her in return, but could not call a blush to her somewhat sallow cheek. Neither could it detract, however, from the delicate prettiness of her refined face with its soft gray shadows, or the dark gentle eyes, whose blue-veined lids were just then wrinkled into coquettishly mischievous lines by the strong light. She was taller and thinner than Kate, and had at times a certain shy, coy sinuosity of movement which gave her a more virginal suggestion than her unmarried sister. For Miss Kate, from her earliest youth, had been distinguished by that matronly sedateness of voice and step, and completeness of figure, which indicates some members of the gallinaceous tribe from their callow infancy.

"I suppose John must have stopped at the Summit on some business," said Mrs. Hale, "or he would have been here already. It's scarcely worth while waiting for him, unless you choose to ride over and meet him. You might change your dress," she continued, looking doubtfully at Kate's costume. "Put on your riding-habit, and take Manuel with you."

"And take the only man we have, and leave you alone?" returned Kate slowly. "No!"

"There are the Chinese field hands," said Mrs. Hale; "you must correct your ideas, and really allow them some humanity, Kate. John says they have a very good compulsory school system in their own country, and can read and write."

"That would be of little use to you here alone if—if—" Kate hesitated.

"If what?" said Mrs. Hale smiling. "Are you thinking of Manuel's dreadful story of the grizzly tracks across the fields this morning? I promise you that neither I, nor mother, nor

Minnie shall stir out of the house until you return, if you wish it."

"I wasn't thinking of that," said Kate; "though I don't believe the beating of a gong and the using of strong language is the best way to frighten a grizzly from the house. Besides, the Chinese are going down the river to-day to a funeral, or a wedding, or a feast of stolen chickens—they're all the same—and won't be here."

"Then take Manuel," repeated Mrs. Hale. "We have the Chinese servants and Indian Molly in the house to protect us from Heaven knows what! I have the greatest confidence in Chy-Lee as a warrior, and in Chinese warfare generally. One has only to hear him pipe in time of peace to imagine what a terror he might become in war time. Indeed, anything more deadly and soul-harrowing than that love song he sang for us last night I cannot conceive. But really, Kate, I am not afraid to stay alone. You know what John says: we ought to be always prepared for anything that might happen.

"My dear Josie," returned Kate, putting her arm around her sister's waist, "I am perfectly convinced that if three-fingered Jack, or two-toed Bill, or even Joaquim Murietta himself, should step, red-handed, on that veranda, you would gently invite him to take a cup of tea, inquire about the state of the road, and refrain delicately from any allusions to the sheriff. But I shan't take Manuel from you. I really cannot undertake to look after his morals at the station, and keep him from drinking aguardiente with suspicious characters at the bar. It is true he 'kisses my hand' in his speech, even when it is thickest, and offers his back to me for a horse-block, but I think I prefer the sober and honest familiarity of even that Pike County landlord who is satisfied to say, 'Jump, girl, and I'll ketch ye!'"

"I hope you didn't change your manner to either of them for that," said Mrs. Hale with a faint sigh. "John wants to be good friends with them, and they are behaving quite decently lately, considering that they can't speak a grammatical sentence nor know the use of a fork."

"And now the man puts on gloves and a tall hat to come here on Sundays, and the woman won't call until you've called first," retorted Kate; "perhaps you call that improvement. The fact is, Josephine," continued the young girl, folding her arms demurely, "we might as well admit it at once—these people don't like us."

"That's impossible!" said Mrs. Hale, with sublime simplicity. "You don't like them, you mean."

"I like them better than you do, Josie, and that's the reason why I feel it and YOU don't." She checked herself, and after a pause resumed in a lighter tone: "No; I sha'n't go to the station; I'll commune with nature to-day, and won't 'take any humanity in mine, thank you,' as Bill the driver says. Adios."

"I wish Kate would not use that dreadful slang, even in jest," said Mrs. Scott, in her rocking-chair at the French window, when Josephine reentered the parlor as her sister walked briskly away. "I am afraid she is being infected by the people at the station. She ought to have a change."

"I was just thinking," said Josephine, looking abstractedly at her mother, "that I would try to get John to take her to San Francisco this winter. The Careys are expected, you know; she might visit them."

"I'm afraid, if she stays here much longer, she won't care to see them at all. She seems to care for nothing now that she ever liked before," returned the old lady ominously.

Meantime the subject of these criticisms was carrying away her own reflections tightly buttoned up in her short jacket. She had driven back her dog Spot—another one of her disillusions, who, giving way to his lower nature, had once killed a sheep—as she did not wish her Jacques-like contemplation of any wounded deer to be inconsistently interrupted by a fresh outrage from her companion. The air was really very chilly, and for the first time in her mountain experience the direct rays of the sun seemed to be shorn of their power. This compelled her to walk more briskly than she was conscious of, for in less than an hour she came suddenly and breathlessly upon the mouth of the canyon, or natural gateway to Eagle's Court.

To her always a profound spectacle of mountain magnificence, it seemed to-day almost terrible in its cold, strong grandeur. The narrowing pass was choked for a moment between two gigantic buttresses of granite, approaching each other so closely at their towering summits that trees growing in opposite clefts of the rock intermingled their branches and pointed the soaring Gothic arch of a stupendous gateway. She raised her eyes with a quickly beating heart. She knew that the interlacing trees above her were as large as those she had just quitted; she knew also that the point where they met was only half-way up the cliff, for she had once gazed down upon them, dwindled to shrubs from the airy summit; she knew that their shaken cones fell a thousand feet perpendicularly, or bounded like shot from the scarred walls they bombarded. She remembered that one of these pines, dislodged from its high foundations, had once dropped like a portcullis in the archway, blocking the pass, and was only carried afterwards by assault of steel and fire. Bending her head mechanically, she ran swiftly through the shadowy passage, and halted only at the beginning of the ascent on the other side.

Bret Harte

It was here that the actual position of the plateau, so indefinite of approach, began to be realized. It now appeared an independent elevation, surrounded on three sides by gorges and watercourses, so narrow as to be overlooked from the principal mountain range, with which it was connected by a long canyon that led to the ridge. At the outlet of this canyon—in bygone ages a mighty river—it had the appearance of having been slowly raised by the diluvium of that river, and the debris washed down from above—a suggestion repeated in miniature by the artificial plateaus of excavated soil raised before the mouths of mining tunnels in the lower flanks of the mountain. It was the realization of a fact—often forgotten by the dwellers in Eagle's Court—that the valley below them, which was their connecting link with the surrounding world, was only reached by ascending the mountain, and the nearest road was over the higher mountain ridge. Never before had this impressed itself so strongly upon the young girl as when she turned that morning to look upon the plateau below her. It seemed to illustrate the conviction that had been slowly shaping itself out of her reflections on the conversation of that morning. It was possible that the perfect understanding of a higher life was only reached from a height still greater, and that to those half-way up the mountain the summit was never as truthfully revealed as to the humbler dwellers in the valley.

I do not know that these profound truths prevented her from gathering some quaint ferns and berries, or from keeping her calm gray eyes open to certain practical changes that were taking place around her. She had noticed a singular thick-ening in the atmosphere that seemed to prevent the passage of the sun's rays, yet without diminishing the transparent quality of the air. The distant snow-peaks were as plainly seen, though they appeared as if in moonlight. This seemed due to no cloud or mist, but rather to a fading of the sun itself. The occasional flurry of wings overhead, the whirring of larger birds in the cover, and a frequent rustling in the undergrowth, as of the passage of some stealthy animal, began equally to attract her attention. It was so different from the habitual silence of these sedate solitudes. Kate had no vague fear of wild beasts; she had been long enough a mountaineer to understand the general immunity enjoyed by the unmolesting wayfarer, and kept her way undismayed. She was descending an abrupt trail when she was stopped by a sudden crash in the bushes. It seemed to come from the opposite incline, directly in a line with her, and apparently on the very trail that she was pursuing. The crash was then repeated again and again lower down, as of a descending body. Expecting the apparition of some fallen tree, or detached boulder bursting through the thicket, in its way to the bottom of the gulch, she waited. The foliage was suddenly brushed aside, and a large grizzly bear half rolled, half waddled, into the trail on the opposite side of the hill. A few moments more would have brought them face to face at the foot of the gulch; when she stopped there were not fifty yards between them.

She did not scream; she did not faint; she was not even frightened. There did not seem to be anything terrifying in this huge, stupid beast, who, arrested by the rustle of a stone displaced by her descending feet, rose slowly on his haunches and gazed at her with small, wondering eyes. Nor did it seem strange to her, seeing that he was in her way, to pick up a stone, throw it in his direction, and say simply, "Sho! get away!" as she would have done to an intruding cow. Nor did it seem odd that he should actually "go away" as he did, scrambling back into the bushes again, and disappearing like some grotesque figure in a transformation scene. It was not until after he had gone that she was taken with a slight nervousness and giddiness, and retraced her steps somewhat hurriedly, shying a little at every rustle in the thicket. By the time she had reached the great gateway she was doubtful whether to be pleased or frightened at the incident, but she concluded to keep it to herself.

It was still intensely cold. The light of the midday sun had decreased still more, and on reaching the plateau again she saw that a dark cloud, not unlike the precursor of a thunder-storm, was brooding over the snowy peaks beyond. In spite of the cold this singular suggestion of summer phenomena was still borne out by the distant smiling valley, and even in the soft grasses at her feet. It seemed to her the crowning inconsistency of the climate, and with a half-serious, half-playful protest on her lips she hurried forward to seek the shelter of the house.

CHAPTER III

To Kate's surprise, the lower part of the house was deserted, but there was an unusual activity on the floor above, and the sound of heavy steps. There were alien marks of dusty feet on the scrupulously clean passage, and on the first step of the stairs a spot of blood. With a sudden genuine alarm that drove her previous adventure from her mind, she impatiently called her sister's name. There was a hasty yet subdued rustle of skirts on the staircase, and Mrs. Hale, with her finger on her lip, swept Kate unceremoniously into the sitting-room, closed the door, and leaned back against it, with a faint smile. She had a crumpled paper in her hand.

"Don't be alarmed, but read that first," she said, handing her sister the paper. "It was brought just now."

Kate instantly recognized her brother's distinct hand. She read hurriedly, "The coach was robbed last night; nobody hurt. I've lost nothing but a day's time, as this business will keep me here until to-morrow, when Manuel can join me with a fresh horse. No cause for alarm. As the bearer goes out of his way to bring you this, see that he wants for nothing."

"Well," said Kate expectantly.

"Well, the 'bearer' was fired upon by the robbers, who were lurking on the Ridge. He was wounded in the leg. Luckily he was picked up by his friend, who was coming to meet him, and brought here as the nearest place. He's up-stairs in the spare bed in the spare room, with his friend, who won't leave his side. He won't even have mother in the room. They've stopped the bleeding with John's ambulance things, and now, Kate, here's a chance for you to show the value of your education in the ambulance class. The ball has got to be extracted. Here's your opportunity."

Kate looked at her sister curiously. There was a faint pink flush on her pale cheeks, and her eyes were gently sparkling. She had never seen her look so pretty before.

"Why not have sent Manuel for a doctor at once?" asked Kate.

"The nearest doctor is fifteen miles away, and Manuel is nowhere to be found. Perhaps he's gone to look after the stock. There's some talk of snow; imagine the absurdity of it!"

"But who are they?"

"They speak of themselves as 'friends,' as if it were a profession. The wounded one was a passenger, I suppose."

"But what are they like?" continued Kate. "I suppose they're like them all."

Mrs. Hale shrugged her shoulders.

"The wounded one, when he's not fainting away, is laughing. The other is a creature with a moustache, and gloomy beyond expression."

"What are you going to do with them?" said Kate.

"What should I do? Even without John's letter I could not refuse the shelter of my house to a wounded and helpless man. I shall keep him, of course, until John comes. Why, Kate, I really believe you are so prejudiced against these people you'd like to turn them out. But I forget! It's because you LIKE them so well. Well, you need not fear to expose yourself to the fascinations of the wounded Christy Minstrel—I'm sure he's that—or to the unspeakable one, who is shyness itself, and would not dare to raise his eyes to you."

There was a timid, hesitating step in the passage. It paused before the door, moved away, returned, and finally asserted its intentions in the gentlest of taps.

"It's him; I'm sure of it," said Mrs. Hale, with a suppressed smile.

Kate threw open the door smartly, to the extreme discomfiture of a tall, dark figure that already had slunk away from it. For all that, he was a good-looking enough fellow, with a moustache as long and almost as flexible as a ringlet. Kate could not help noticing also that his hand, which was nervously pulling the moustache, was white and thin.

"Excuse me," he stammered, without raising his eyes, "I was looking for—for—the old lady. I—I beg your pardon. I didn't know that you—the young ladies—company—were here. I intended—I only wanted to say that my friend—" He stopped at the slight smile that passed quickly over Mrs. Hale's mouth, and his pale face reddened with an angry flush.

"I hope he is not worse," said Mrs. Hale, with more than her usual languid gentleness. "My mother is not here at present.

Can I—can WE—this is my sister—do as well?"

Without looking up he made a constrained recognition of Kate's presence, that embarrassed and curt as it was, had none of the awkwardness of rusticity.

"Thank you; you're very kind. But my friend is a little stronger, and if you can lend me an extra horse I'll try to get him on the Summit to-night."

"But you surely will not take him away from us so soon?" said Mrs. Hale, with a languid look of alarm, in which Kate, however, detected a certain real feeling. "Wait at least until my husband returns to-morrow."

"He won't be here to-morrow," said the stranger hastily. He stopped, and as quickly corrected himself. "That is, his business is so very uncertain, my friend says."

Only Kate noticed the slip; but she noticed also that her sister was apparently unconscious of it. "You think," she said, "that Mr. Hale may be delayed?"

He turned upon her almost brusquely. "I mean that it is already snowing up there;" he pointed through the window to the cloud Kate had noticed; "if it comes down lower in the pass the roads will be blocked up. That is why it would be better for us to try and get on at once."

"But if Mr. Hale is likely to be stopped by snow, so are you," said Mrs. Hale playfully; "and you had better let us try to make your friend comfortable here rather than expose him to that uncertainty in his weak condition. We will do our best for him. My sister is dying for an opportunity to show her skill in surgery," she continued, with an unexpected mischievousness that only added to Kate's surprised embarrassment.

"Aren't you, Kate?"

Equivocal as the young girl knew her silence appeared, she was unable to utter the simplest polite evasion. Some unaccountable impulse kept her constrained and speechless. The stranger did not, however, wait for her reply, but, casting a swift, hurried glance around the room, said, "It's impossible; we must go. In fact, I've already taken the liberty to order the horses round. They are at the door now. You may be certain," he added, with quick earnestness, suddenly lifting his dark eyes to Mrs. Hale, and as rapidly withdrawing them, "that your horse will be returned at once, and—and—we won't forget your kindness." He stopped and turned towards the hall. "I—I have brought my friend downstairs. He wants to thank you before he goes."

As he remained standing in the hall the two women stepped to the door. To their surprise, half reclining on a cane sofa was the wounded man, and what could be seen of his slight figure was wrapped in a dark serape. His beardless face gave him a quaint boyishness quite inconsistent with the mature lines of his temples and forehead. Pale, and in pain, as he evidently was, his blue eyes twinkled with intense amusement. Not only did his manner offer a marked contrast to the sombre uneasiness of his companion, but he seemed to be the only one perfectly at his ease in the group around him.

"It's rather rough making you come out here to see me off," he said, with a not unmusical laugh that was very infectious, "but Ned there, who carried me downstairs, wanted to tote me round the house in his arms like a baby to say ta-ta to you all. Excuse my not rising, but I feel as uncertain below as a mermaid, and as out of my element," he added, with a mischievous glance at his friend. "Ned concluded I must go on. But I must say good-by to the old lady first. Ah! here she is."

To Kate's complete bewilderment, not only did the utter familiarity of this speech, pass unnoticed and unrebuked by her sister, but actually her own mother advanced quickly with every expression of lively sympathy, and with the authority of her years and an almost maternal anxiety endeavored to dissuade the invalid from going. "This is not my house," she said, looking at her daughter, "but if it were I should not hear of your leaving, not only to-night, but until you were out of danger. Josephine! Kate! What are you thinking of to permit it? Well, then I forbid it—there!"

Had they become suddenly insane, or were they bewitched by this morose intruder and his insufferably familiar confidant? The man was wounded, it was true; they might have to put him up in common humanity; but here was her austere mother, who wouldn't come in the room when Whisky Dick called on business, actually pressing both of the invalid's hands, while her sister, who never extended a finger to the ordinary visiting humanity of the neighborhood, looked on with evident complacency.

The wounded man suddenly raised Mrs. Scott's hand to his lips, kissed it gently, and, with his smile quite vanished, endeavored to rise to his feet. "It's of no use—we must go. Give me your arm, Ned. Quick! Are the horses there?"

"Dear me," said Mrs. Scott quickly. "I forgot to say the horse cannot be found anywhere. Manuel must have taken him this morning to look up the stock. But he will be back to-night certainly, and if to-morrow—"

The wounded man sank back to a sitting position. "Is Manuel your man?" he asked grimly.

"Yes."

The two men exchanged glances.

"Marked on his left cheek and drinks a good deal?"

"Yes," said Kate, finding her voice. "Why?"

The amused look came back to the man's eyes. "That kind of man isn't safe to wait for. We must take our own horse, Ned. Are you ready?"

"Yes."

The wounded man again attempted to rise. He fell back, but this time quite heavily. He had fainted.

Involuntarily and simultaneously the three women rushed to his side. "He cannot go," said Kate suddenly.

"He will be better in a moment."

"But only for a moment. Will nothing induce you to change your mind?"

As if in reply a sudden gust of wind brought a volley of rain against the window.

"THAT will," said the stranger bitterly.

"The rain?"

"A mile from here it is SNOW; and before we could reach the Summit with these horses the road would be impassable."

He made a slight gesture to himself, as if accepting an inevitable defeat, and turned to his companion, who was slowly reviving under the active ministration of the two women.

The wounded man looked around with a weak smile. "This is one way of going off," he said faintly, "but I could do this sort of thing as well on the road."

"You can do nothing now," said his friend, decidedly. "Before we get to the Gate the road will be impassable for our horses."

"For ANY horses?" asked Kate.

"For any horses. For any man or beast I might say. Where we cannot get out, no one can get in," he added, as if answering her thoughts. "I am afraid that you won't see your brother tomorrow morning. But I'll reconnoitre as soon as I can do so without torturing HIM," he said, looking anxiously at the helpless man; "he's got about his share of pain, I reckon, and the first thing is to get him easier." It was the longest speech he had made to her; it was the first time he had fairly looked her in the face. His shy restlessness had suddenly given way to dogged resignation, less abstracted, but scarcely more flattering to his entertainers. Lifting his companion gently in his arms, as if he had been a child, he reascended the staircase, Mrs. Scott and the hastily-summoned Molly following with overflowing solicitude. As soon as they were alone in the parlor Mrs. Hale turned to her sister: "Only that our guests seemed to be as anxious to go just now as you were to pack them off, I should have been shocked at your inhospitality. What has come over you, Kate? These are the very people you have reproached me so often with not being civil enough to."

"But WHO are they?"

"How do I know? There is YOUR BROTHER'S letter."

She usually spoke of her husband as "John." This slight

shifting of relationship and responsibility to the feminine mind was significant. Kate was a little frightened and remorseful.

"I only meant you don't even know their names."

"That wasn't necessary for giving them a bed and bandages. Do you suppose the good Samaritan ever asked the wounded Jew's name, and that the Levite did not excuse himself because the thieves had taken the poor man's card-case? Do the directions, 'In case of accident,' in your ambulance rules, read, 'First lay the sufferer on his back and inquire his name and family connections'? Besides, you can call one 'Ned' and the other 'George,' if you like."

"Oh, you know what I mean," said Kate, irrelevantly. "Which is George?"

"George is the wounded man," said Mrs. Hale; "NOT the one who talked to you more than he did to any one else. I suppose the poor man was frightened and read dismissal in your eyes."

"I wish John were here."

"I don't think we have anything to fear in his absence from men whose only wish is to get away from us. If it is a question of propriety, my dear Kate, surely there is the presence of mother to prevent any scandal—although really her own conduct with the wounded one is not above suspicion," she added, with that novel mischievousness that seemed a return of her lost girlhood. "We must try to do the best we can with them and for them," she said decidedly, "and meantime I'll see if I can't arrange John's room for them."

"John's room?"

"Oh, mother is perfectly satisfied; indeed, suggested it. It's larger and will hold two beds, for 'Ned,' the friend, must attend to him at night. And, Kate, don't you think, if you're not going out again, you might change your costume? It does very well while we are alone—"

"Well," said Kate indignantly, "as I am not going into his room—"

"I'm not so sure about that, if we can't get a regular doctor. But he is very restless, and wanders all over the house like a timid and apologetic spaniel."

"Who?"

"Why 'Ned.' But I must go and look after the patient. I suppose they've got him safe in his bed again," and with a nod to her sister she tripped up-stairs.

Uncomfortable and embarrassed, she knew not why, Kate sought her mother. But that good lady was already in attendance on the patient, and Kate hurried past that baleful centre of attraction with a feeling of loneliness and strangeness she had never experienced before. Entering her own room she went to the window—that first and last refuge of the troubled mind—and gazed out. Turning her eyes in the direction of her morning's walk, she started back with a sense of being dazzled. She rubbed first her eyes and then the rain-dimmed pane. It was no illusion! The whole landscape, so familiar to her, was one vast field of dead, colorless white! Trees, rocks, even distance itself, had vanished in those few hours. An even shadowless, motionless white sea filled the horizon. On either side a vast wall of snow seemed to shut out the world like a shroud. Only the green plateau before her, with its sloping meadows and fringe of pines and cotton-wood, lay alone like a summer island in this frozen sea.

A sudden desire to view this phenomenon more closely, and to learn for herself the limits of this new tethered life, completely possessed her, and, accustomed to act upon her independent impulses, she seized a hooded waterproof cloak, and slipped out of the house unperceived. The rain was falling steadily along the descending trail where she walked, but beyond, scarcely a mile across the chasm, the wintry distance began to confuse her brain with the inextricable swarming of snow. Hurrying down with feverish excitement, she at last came in sight of the arching granite portals of their domain. But her first glance through the gateway showed it closed as if with a white portcullis. Kate remembered that the trail began to ascend beyond the arch, and knew that what she saw was only the mountain side she had partly climbed this morning. But the snow had already crept down its flank, and the exit by trail was practically closed. Breathlessly making her way back to the highest part of the plateau—the cliff behind the house that here descended abruptly to the rain-dimmed valley—she gazed at the dizzy depths in vain for some undiscovered or forgotten trail along its face. But a single glance convinced her of its inaccessibility. The gateway was indeed their only outlet to the plain below. She looked back at the falling snow beyond until she fancied she could see in the crossing and recrossing lines the moving meshes of a fateful web woven around them by viewless but inexorable fingers.

Half frightened, she was turning away, when she perceived, a few paces distant, the figure of the stranger, "Ned," also apparently absorbed in the gloomy prospect. He was wrapped in the clinging folds of a black serape braided with silver; the broad flap of a slouch hat beaten back by the wind exposed the dark, glistening curls on his white forehead. He was certainly very handsome and picturesque, and that apparently without effort or consciousness. Neither was there anything in his costume or appearance inconsistent with his surroundings, or, even with what Kate could judge were his habits or position. Nevertheless, she instantly decided that he was TOO handsome and too picturesque, without suspecting that her ideas of the limits of masculine beauty were merely personal experience.

As he turned away from the cliff they were brought face to face. "It doesn't look very encouraging over there," he said quietly, as if the inevitableness of the situation had relieved him of his previous shyness and effort; "it's even worse than I expected. The snow must have begun there last night, and it looks as if it meant to stay." He stopped for a moment, and then, lifting his eyes to her, said:—

"I suppose you know what this means?"

"I don't understand you."

"I thought not. Well! it means that you are absolutely cut off here from any communication or intercourse with any one outside of that canyon. By this time the snow is five feet deep over the only trail by which one can pass in and out of that gateway. I am not alarming you, I hope, for there is no real physical danger; a place like this ought to be well garrisoned, and certainly is self-supporting so far as the mere necessities and even comforts are concerned. You have wood, water, cattle, and game at your command, but for two weeks at least you are completely isolated."

"For two weeks," said Kate, growing pale—"and my brother!"

"He knows all by this time, and is probably as assured as I

am of the safety of his family."

"For two weeks," continued Kate; "impossible! You don't know my brother! He will find some way to get to us."

"I hope so," returned the stranger gravely, "for what is possible for him is possible for us."

"Then you are anxious to get away," Kate could not help saying.

"Very."

The reply was not discourteous in manner, but was so far from gallant that Kate felt a new and inconsistent resentment. Before she could say anything he added, "And I hope you will remember, whatever may happen, that I did my best to avoid staying here longer than was necessary to keep my friend from bleeding to death in the road."

"Certainly," said Kate; then added awkwardly, "I hope he'll be better soon." She was silent, and then, quickening her pace, said hurriedly, "I must tell my sister this dreadful news."

"I think she is prepared for it. If there is anything I can do to help you I hope you will let me know. Perhaps I may be of some service. I shall begin by exploring the trails to-morrow, for the best service we can do you possibly is to take ourselves off; but I can carry a gun, and the woods are full of game driven down from the mountains. Let me show you something you may not have noticed." He stopped, and pointed to a small knoll of sheltered shrubbery and granite on the opposite mountain, which still remained black against the surrounding snow. It seemed to be thickly covered with moving objects. "They are wild animals driven out of the snow," said the stranger. "That larger one is a grizzly; there is a panther, wolves, wild cats, a fox, and some mountain goats."

"An ill-assorted party," said the young girl.

"Ill luck makes them companions. They are too frightened to hurt one another now."

"But they will eat each other later on," said Kate, stealing a glance at her companion.

He lifted his long lashes and met her eyes. "Not on a haven of refuge."

CHAPTER IV

Kate found her sister, as the stranger had intimated, fully prepared. A hasty inventory of provisions and means of subsistence showed that they had ample resources for a much longer isolation.

"They tell me it is by no means an uncommon case, Kate; somebody over at somebody's place was snowed in for four weeks, and now it appears that even the Summit House is not always accessible. John ought to have known it when he bought the place; in fact, I was ashamed to admit that he did not. But that is like John to prefer his own theories to the experience of others. However, I don't suppose we should even notice the privation except for the mails. It will be a lesson to John, though. As Mr. Lee says, he is on the outside, and can probably go wherever he likes from the Summit except to come here."

"Mr. Lee?" echoed Kate.

"Yes, the wounded one; and the other's name is Falkner. I asked them in order that you might be properly introduced. There were very respectable Falkners in Charlestown, you remember; I thought you might warm to the name, and perhaps trace the connection, now that you are such good friends. It's providential they are here, as we haven't got a horse or a man in the place since Manuel disappeared, though Mr. Falkner says he can't be far away, or they would have met him on the trail if he had gone towards the Summit."

"Did they say anything more of Manuel?"

"Nothing; though I am inclined to agree with you that he isn't trustworthy. But that again is the result of John's idea of employing native skill at the expense of retaining native habits."

The evening closed early, and with no diminution in the falling rain and rising wind. Falkner kept his word, and unostentatiously performed the out-door work in the barn and stables, assisted by the only Chinese servant remaining, and under the advice and supervision of Kate. Although he seemed to understand horses, she was surprised to find that he betrayed a civic ignorance of the ordinary details of the farm and rustic household. It was quite impossible that she should retain her distrustful attitude, or he his reserve in their enforced companionship. They talked freely of subjects suggested by the situation, Falkner exhibiting a general knowledge and intuition of things without parade or dogmatism. Doubtful of all versatility as Kate was, she could not help admitting to herself that his truths were none the less true for their quantity or that he got at them without ostentatious processes. His talk certainly was more picturesque than her brother's, and less subduing to her faculties. John had always crushed her.

When they returned to the house he did not linger in the parlor or sitting-room, but at once rejoined his friend. When dinner was ready in the dining-room, a little more deliberately arranged and ornamented than usual, the two women were somewhat surprised to receive an excuse from

Falkner, begging them to allow him for the present to take his meals with the patient, and thus save the necessity of another attendant.

"It is all shyness, Kate," said Mrs. Hale, confidently, "and must not be permitted for a moment."

"I'm sure I should be quite willing to stay with the poor boy myself," said Mrs. Scott, simply, "and take Mr. Falkner's place while he dines."

"You are too willing, mother," said Mrs. Hale, pertly, "and your 'poor boy,' as you call him, will never see thirty-five again."

"He will never see any other birthday!" retorted her mother, "unless you keep him more quiet. He only talks when you're in the room."

"He wants some relief to his friend's long face and moustachios that make him look prematurely in mourning," said Mrs. Hale, with a slight increase of animation. "I don't propose to leave them too much together. After dinner we'll adjourn to their room and lighten it up a little. You must come, Kate, to look at the patient, and counteract the baleful effects of my frivolity."

Mrs. Hale's instincts were truer than her mother's experience; not only that the wounded man's eyes became brighter under the provocation of her presence, but it was evident that his naturally exuberant spirits were a part of his vital strength, and were absolutely essential to his quick recovery. Encouraged by Falkner's grave and practical assistance, which she could not ignore, Kate ventured to make an examination of Lee's wound. Even to her unpractised eye it was less serious than at first appeared. The great loss of blood had been due to the laceration of certain small vessels below the knee, but neither artery nor bone was injured. A recurrence of the haemorrhage or fever was the only thing to be feared, and these could be averted by bandaging, repose, and simple nursing.

The unfailing good humor of the patient under this manipulation, the quaint originality of his speech, the freedom of his fancy, which was, however, always controlled by a certain instinctive tact, began to affect Kate nearly as it had the others. She found herself laughing over the work she had undertaken in a pure sense of duty; she joined in the hilarity produced by Lee's affected terror of her surgical mania, and offered to undo the bandages in search of the thimble he declared she had left in the wound with a view to further experiments.

"You ought to broaden your practice," he suggested. "A good deal might be made out of Ned and a piece of soap left carelessly on the first step of the staircase, while mountains of surgical opportunities lie in a humble orange peel judiciously exposed. Only I warn you that you wouldn't find him as docile as I am. Decoyed into a snow-drift and frozen, you might get some valuable experiences in resuscitation by thawing him."

"I fancied you had done that already, Kate," whispered Mrs. Hale.

"Freezing is the new suggestion for painless surgery," said Lee, coming to Kate's relief with ready tact, "only the knowledge should be more generally spread. There was a man up at Strawberry fell under a sledge-load of wood in the snow. Stunned by the shock, he was slowly freezing to death, when, with a tremendous effort, he succeeded in freeing himself all but his right leg, pinned down by a small log. His axe happened to have fallen within reach, and a few blows on the log freed him."

"And saved the poor fellow's life," said Mrs. Scott, who was listening with sympathizing intensity.

"At the expense of his LEFT LEG, which he had unknowingly cut off under the pleasing supposition that it was a log," returned Lee demurely.

Nevertheless, in a few moments he managed to divert the slightly shocked susceptibilities of the old lady with some raillery of himself, and did not again interrupt the even good-humored communion of the party. The rain beating against the windows and the fire sparkling on the hearth seemed to lend a charm to their peculiar isolation, and it was not until Mrs. Scott rose with a warning that they were trespassing upon the rest of their patient that they discovered that the evening had slipped by unnoticed. When the door at last closed on the bright, sympathetic eyes of the two young women and the motherly benediction of the elder, Falkner walked to the window, and remained silent, looking into the darkness. Suddenly he turned bitterly to his companion.

"This is just h-ll, George."

George Lee, with a smile on his boyish face, lazily moved his head.

"I don't know! If it wasn't for the old woman, who is the one solid chunk of absolute goodness here, expecting nothing, wanting nothing, it would be good fun enough! These two women, cooped up in this house, wanted excitement. They've got it! That man Hale wanted to show off by going for us; he's had his chance, and will have it again before I've done with him. That d—d fool of a messenger wanted to go out of his way to exchange shots with me; I reckon he's the most satisfied of the lot! I don't know why YOU should growl. You did your level best to get away from here, and the result is, that little Puritan is ready to worship you."

"Yes—but this playing it on them—George—this—"

"Who's playing it? Not you; I see you've given away our names already."

"I couldn't lie, and they know nothing by that."

"Do you think they would be happier by knowing it? Do you think that soft little creature would be as happy as she was to-night if she knew that her husband had been indirectly the means of laying me by the heels here? Where is the swindle? This hole in my leg? If you had been five minutes under that girl's d—d sympathetic fingers you'd have thought it was genuine. Is it in our trying to get away? Do you call that ten-feet drift in the pass a swindle? Is it in the chance of Hale getting back while we're here? That's real enough, isn't it? I say, Ned, did you ever give your unfettered intellect to the contemplation of THAT?"

Falkner did not reply. There was an interval of silence, but he could see from the movement of George's shoulders that he was shaking with suppressed laughter.

"Fancy Mrs. Hale archly introducing her husband! My offering him a chair, but being all the time obliged to cover him with a derringer under the bedclothes. Your rushing in from your peaceful pastoral pursuits in the barn, with a pitchfork in one hand and the girl in the other, and dear old mammy sympathizing all round and trying to make everything comfortable."

"I should not be alive to see it, George," said Falkner gloomily.

"You'd manage to pitchfork me and those two women on Hale's horse and ride away; that's what you'd do, or I don't know you! Look here, Ned," he added more seriously, "the only swindling was our bringing that note here. That was YOUR idea. You thought it would remove suspicion, and as you believed I was bleeding to death you played that game for all it was worth to save me. You might have done what I asked you to do—propped me up in the bushes, and got away yourself. I was good for a couple of shots yet, and after that—what mattered? That night, the next day, the next time I take the road, or a year hence? It will come when it will come, all the same!"

He did not speak bitterly, nor relax his smile. Falkner, without speaking, slid his hand along the coverlet. Lee grasped it, and their hands remained clasped together for a few minutes in silence.

"How is this to end? We cannot go on here in this way," said Falkner suddenly.

"If we cannot get away it must go on. Look here, Ned. I don't reckon to take anything out of this house that I didn't bring in it, or isn't freely offered to me; yet I don't otherwise, you understand, intend making myself out a d—d bit better than I am. That's the only excuse I have for not making myself out JUST WHAT I am. I don't know the fellow who's obliged to tell every one the last company he was in, or the last thing he did! Do you suppose even these pretty little women tell US their whole story? Do you fancy that this St. John in the wilderness is canonized in his family? Perhaps, when I take the liberty to intrude in his affairs, as he has in mine, he'd see he isn't. I don't blame you for being sensitive, Ned. It's natural. When a man lives outside the revised statutes of his own State he is apt to be awfully fine on points of etiquette in his own household. As for me, I find it rather comfortable here. The beds of other people's making strike me as being more satisfactory than my own. Good-night."

In a few moments he was sleeping the peaceful sleep of that youth which seemed to be his own dominant quality. Falkner stood for a little space and watched him, following the boyish lines of his cheek on the pillow, from the shadow of the light brown lashes under his closed lids to the lifting of his short upper lip over his white teeth, with his regular respiration. Only a sharp accenting of the line of nostril and jaw and a faint depression of the temple betrayed his already tried manhood.

The house had long sunk to repose when Falkner returned to the window, and remained looking out upon the storm. Suddenly he extinguished the light, and passing quickly to the bed laid his hand upon the sleeper. Lee opened his eyes instantly.

"Are you awake?"

"Perfectly."

"Somebody is trying to get into the house!"

"Not HIM, eh?" said Lee gayly.

"No; two men. Mexicans, I think. One looks like Manuel."

"Ah," said Lee, drawing himself up to a sitting posture.

"Well?"

"Don't you see? He believes the women are alone."

"The dog—d—d hound!"

"Speak respectfully of one of my people, if you please, and hand me my derringer. Light the candle again, and open the door. Let them get in quietly. They'll come here first. It's HIS room, you understand, and if there's any money it's here. Anyway, they must pass here to get to the women's rooms. Leave Manuel to me, and you take care of the other."

"I see."

"Manuel knows the house, and will come first. When he's fairly in the room shut the door and go for the other. But no noise. This is just one of the SW-EETEST things out—if it's done properly."

"But YOU, George?"

"If I couldn't manage that fellow without turning down the bedclothes I'd kick myself. Hush. Steady now."

He lay down and shut his eyes as if in natural repose. Only his right hand, carelessly placed under his pillow, closed on the handle of his pistol. Falkner quietly slipped into the passage. The light of the candle faintly illuminated the floor and opposite wall, but left it on either side in pitchy obscurity.

For some moments the silence was broken only by the sound of the rain without. The recumbent figure in bed seemed to have actually succumbed to sleep. The multitudinous small noises of a house in repose might have been misinterpreted by ears less keen than the sleeper's; but when the apparent creaking of a far-off shutter was followed by the sliding apparition of a dark head of tangled hair at the door, Lee had not been deceived, and was as prepared as if he had seen it. Another step, and the figure entered the room. The door closed instantly behind it. The sound of a heavy body struggling against the partition outside followed, and then suddenly ceased.

The intruder turned, and violently grasped the handle of the door, but recoiled at a quiet voice from the bed.

"Drop that, and come here."

He started back with an exclamation. The sleeper's eyes were wide open; the sleeper's extended arm and pistol covered him.

"Silence! or I'll let that candle shine through you!"

"Yes, captain!" growled the astounded and frightened half-breed. "I didn't know you were here."

Lee raised himself, and grasped the long whip in his left hand and whirled it round his head.

"WILL YOU dry up?"

The man sank back against the wall in silent terror.

"Open that door now—softly."

Manuel obeyed with trembling fingers.

"Ned" said Lee in a low voice, "bring him in here—quick."

There was a slight rustle, and Falkner appeared, backing in another gasping figure, whose eyes were starting under the strong grasp of the captor at his throat.

"Silence," said Lee, "all of you."

There was a breathless pause. The sound of a door hesitatingly opened in the passage broke the stillness, followed by the gentle voice of Mrs. Scott.

"Is anything the matter?"

Lee made a slight gesture of warning to Falkner, of menace to the others. "Everything's the matter," he called out cheerily. "Ned's managed to half pull down the house trying to get at something from my saddle-bags."

"I hope he has not hurt himself," broke in another voice mischievously.

"Answer, you clumsy villain," whispered Lee, with twinkling eyes.

"I'm all right, thank you," responded Falkner, with unaffected awkwardness.

There was a slight murmuring of voices, and then the door was heard to close. Lee turned to Falkner.

"Disarm that hound and turn him loose outside, and make no noise. And you, Manuel! tell him what his and your chances are if he shows his black face here again."

Manuel cast a single, terrified, supplicating glance, more suggestive than words, at his confederate, as Falkner shoved him before him from the room. The next moment they were silently descending the stairs.

"May I go too, captain?" entreated Manuel. "I swear to God—"

"Shut the door!" The man obeyed.

"Now, then," said Lee, with a broad, gratified smile, laying down his whip and pistol within reach, and comfortably settling the pillows behind his back, "we'll have a quiet confab. A sort of old-fashioned talk, eh? You're not looking well, Manuel. You're drinking too much again. It spoils your complexion."

"Let me go, captain," pleaded the man, emboldened by the good-humored voice, but not near enough to notice a peculiar light in the speaker's eye.

"You've only just come, Manuel; and at considerable trouble, too. Well, what have you got to say? What's all this about? What are you doing here?"

The captured man shuffled his feet nervously, and only uttered an uneasy laugh of coarse discomfiture.

"I see. You're bashful. Well, I'll help you along. Come! You knew that Hale was away and these women were here without a man to help them. You thought you'd find some money here, and have your own way generally, eh?"

The tone of Lee's voice inspired him to confidence; unfortunately, it inspired him with familiarity also.

"I reckoned I had the right to a little fun on my own account, cap. I reckoned ez one gentleman in the profession wouldn't interfere with another gentleman's little game," he continued coarsely.

"Stand up."

"Wot for?"

"Up, I say!"

Manuel stood up and glanced at him.

"Utter a cry that might frighten these women, and by the living God they'll rush in here only to find you lying dead on the floor of the house you'd have polluted."

He grasped the whip and laid the lash of it heavily twice over the ruffian's shoulders. Writhing in suppressed agony, the man fell imploringly on his knees.

"Now, listen!" said Lee, softly twirling the whip in the air. "I want to refresh your memory. Did you ever learn, when you were with me—before I was obliged to kick you out of gentlemen's company—to break into a private house? Answer!"

"No," stammered the wretch.

"Did you ever learn to rob a woman, a child, or any but a man, and that face to face?"

"No," repeated Manuel.

"Did you ever learn from me to lay a finger upon a woman, old or young, in anger or kindness?"

"No."

"Then, my poor Manuel, it's as I feared; civilization has ruined you. Farming and a simple, bucolic life have perverted your morals. So you were running off with the stock and that mustang, when you got stuck in the snow; and the luminous idea of this little game struck you? Eh? That was another mistake, Manuel; I never allowed you to think when you were with me."

"No, captain."

"Who's your friend?"

"A d—d cowardly nigger from the Summit."

"I agree with you for once; but he hasn't had a very brilliant example. Where's he gone now?"

"To h-ll, for all I care!"

"Then I want you to go with him. Listen. If there's a way out of the place, you know it or can find it. I give you two days to do it—you and he. At the end of that time the order will be to shoot you on sight. Now take off your boots."

The man's dark face visibly whitened, his teeth chattered in superstitious terror.

"I'm not going to shoot you now," said Lee, smiling, "so you will have a chance to die with your boots on,* if you are superstitious. I only want you to exchange them for that pair of Hale's in the corner. The fact is I have taken a fancy to yours. That fashion of wearing the stockings outside strikes me as one of the neatest things out."

* "To die with one's boots on." A synonym for death by violence, popular among Southwestern desperadoes, and the subject of superstitious dread.

Manuel suddenly drew off his boots with their muffled covering, and put on the ones designated.

"Now open the door."

He did so. Falkner was already waiting at the threshold, "Turn Manuel loose with the other, Ned, but disarm him first. They might quarrel. The habit of carrying arms, Manuel," added Lee, as Falkner took a pistol and bowie-knife from the half-breed, "is of itself provocative of violence, and inconsistent with a bucolic and pastoral life."

When Falkner returned he said hurriedly to his companion, "Do you think it wise, George, to let those hell-hounds loose? Good God! I could scarcely let my grip of his throat go, when I thought of what they were hunting."

"My dear Ned," said Lee, luxuriously ensconcing himself under the bedclothes again with a slight shiver of delicious warmth, "I must warn you against allowing the natural pride of a higher walk to prejudice you against the general level of our profession. Indeed, I was quite struck with the justice of Manuel's protest that I was interfering with certain rude processes of his own towards results aimed at by others."

"George!" interrupted Falkner, almost savagely.

"Well. I admit it's getting rather late in the evening for pure philosophical inquiry, and you are tired. Practically, then, it WAS wise to let them get away before they discovered two things. One, our exact relations here with these women; and the other, HOW MANY of us were here. At present they think we are three or four in possession and with the consent of the women."

"The dogs!"

"They are paying us the highest compliment they can conceive of by supposing us cleverer scoundrels than themselves. You are very unjust, Ned."

"If they escape and tell their story?"

"We shall have the rare pleasure of knowing we are better than people believe us. And now put those boots away somewhere where we can produce them if necessary, as evidence of Manuel's evening call. At present we'll keep the thing quiet, and in the early morning you can find out where they got in and remove any traces they have left. It is no use to frighten the women. There's no fear of their returning."

"And if they get away?"

"We can follow in their tracks."

"If Manuel gives the alarm?"

"With his burglarious boots left behind in the house? Not much! Good-night, Ned. Go to bed."

With these words Lee turned on his side and quietly resumed his interrupted slumber. Falkner did not, however, follow this sensible advice. When he was satisfied that his friend was sleeping he opened the door softly and looked out. He did not appear to be listening, for his eyes were fixed upon a small pencil of light that stole across the passage from the foot of Kate's door. He watched it until it suddenly disappeared, when, leaving the door partly open, he threw himself on his couch without removing his clothes. The slight movement awakened the sleeper, who was beginning to feel the accession of fever. He moved restlessly.

"George," said Falkner, softly.

"Yes."

"Where was it we passed that old Mission Church on the road one dark night, and saw the light burning before the figure of the Virgin through the window?"

There was a moment of crushing silence. "Does that mean you're wanting to light the candle again?"

"No."

"Then don't lie there inventing sacrilegious conundrums, but go to sleep."

Nevertheless, in the morning his fever was slightly worse. Mrs. Hale, offering her condolence, said, "I know that you have not been resting well, for even after your friend met with that mishap in the hall, I heard your voices, and Kate says your door was open all night. You have a little fever too, Mr. Falkner."

George looked curiously at Falkner's pale face—it was burning.

CHAPTER V

The speed and fury with which Clinch's cavalcade swept on in the direction of the mysterious shot left Hale no chance for reflection. He was conscious of shouting incoherently with the others, of urging his horse irresistibly forward, of momentarily expecting to meet or overtake something, but without any further thought. The figures of Clinch and Rawlins immediately before him shut out the prospect of the narrowing trail. Once only, taking advantage of a sudden halt that threw them confusedly together, he managed to ask a question.

"Lost their track—found it again!" shouted the ostler, as Clinch, with a cry like the baying of a hound, again darted forward. Their horses were panting and trembling under them, the ascent seemed to be growing steeper, a singular darkness, which even the density of the wood did not sufficiently account for, surrounded them, but still their leader madly urged them on. To Hale's returning senses they did not seem in a condition to engage a single resolute man, who might have ambushed in the woods or beaten them in detail in the narrow gorge, but in another instant the reason of their furious haste was manifest. Spurring his horse ahead, Clinch dashed out into the open with a cheering shout—a shout that as quickly changed to a yell of imprecation. They were on the Ridge in a blinding snow-storm! The road had already vanished under their feet, and with it the fresh trail they had so closely followed! They stood helplessly on the shore of a trackless white sea, blank and spotless of any trace or sign of the fugitives.

"'Pears to me, boys," said the ostler, suddenly ranging before them, "ef you're not kalkilatin' on gittin' another party to dig ye out, ye'd better be huntin' fodder and cover instead of road agents. 'Skuse me, gentlemen, but I'm responsible for the hosses, and this ain't no time for circus-ridin'. We're a matter o' six miles from the station in a bee line."

"Back to the trail, then," said Clinch, wheeling his horse towards the road they had just quitted.

"'Skuse me, Kernel," said the ostler, laying his hand on Clinch's rein, "but that way only brings us back the road we kem—the stage road—three miles further from home. That three miles is on the divide, and by the time we get there it will be snowed up worse nor this. The shortest cut is along the Ridge. If we hump ourselves we ken cross the divide afore the road is blocked. And that, 'skuse me, gentlemen, is MY road."

There was no time for discussion. The road was already palpably thickening under their feet. Hale's arm was stiffened to his side by a wet, clinging snow-wreath. The figures of the others were almost obliterated and shapeless. It was not snowing—it was snowballing! The huge flakes, shaken like enormous feathers out of a vast blue-black cloud, commingled and fell in sprays and patches. All idea of their former pursuit was forgotten; the blind rage and enthusiasm that had possessed them was gone. They dashed after their new leader with only an instinct for shelter and succor.

They had not ridden long when fortunately, as it seemed to

Bret Harte

Hale, the character of the storm changed. The snow no longer fell in such large flakes, nor as heavily. A bitter wind succeeded; the soft snow began to stiffen and crackle under the horses' hoofs; they were no longer weighted and encumbered by the drifts upon their bodies; the smaller flakes now rustled and rasped against them like sand, or bounded from them like hail. They seemed to be moving more easily and rapidly, their spirits were rising with the stimulus of cold and motion, when suddenly their leader halted.

"It's no use, boys. It can't be done! This is no blizzard, but a regular two days' snifter! It's no longer meltin', but packin' and driftin' now. Even if we get over the divide, we're sure to be blocked up in the pass."

It was true! To their bitter disappointment they could now see that the snow had not really diminished in quantity, but that the now finely-powdered particles were rapidly filling all inequalities of the surface, packing closely against projections, and swirling in long furrows across the levels. They looked with anxiety at their self-constituted leader.

"We must make a break to get down in the woods again before it's too late," he said briefly.

But they had already drifted away from the fringe of larches and dwarf pines that marked the sides of the Ridge, and lower down merged into the dense forest that clothed the flank of the mountain they had lately climbed, and it was with the greatest difficulty that they again reached it, only to find that at that point it was too precipitous for the descent of their horses. Benumbed and speechless, they continued to toil on, opposed to the full fury of the stinging snow, and at times obliged to turn their horses to the blast to keep from being blown over the Ridge. At the end of half an hour the ostler dismounted, and, beckoning to the others, took his horse by the bridle, and began the descent. When it came to Hale's turn to dismount he could not help at first recoiling from the prospect before him. The trail—if it could be so called—was merely the track or furrow of some fallen tree dragged, by accident or design, diagonally across the sides of the mountain. At times it appeared scarcely a foot in width; at other times a mere crumbling gully, or a narrow shelf made by the projections of dead boughs and collected debris. It seemed perilous for a foot passenger, it appeared impossible for a horse. Nevertheless, he had taken a step forward when Clinch laid his hand on his arm.

"You'll bring up the rear," he said not unkindly, "ez you're a stranger here. Wait until we sing out to you."

"But if I prefer to take the same risks as you all?" said Hale stiffly.

"You kin," said Clinch grimly. "But I reckoned, as you wern't familiar with this sort o' thing, you wouldn't keer, by any foolishness o' yours, to stampede the rocks ahead of us, and break down the trail, or send down an avalanche on top of us. But just ez you like."

"I will wait, then," said Hale hastily.

The rebuke, however, did him good service. It preoccupied his mind, so that it remained unaffected by the dizzy depths, and enabled him to abandon himself mechanically to the sagacity of his horse, who was contented simply to follow the hoofprints of the preceding animal, and in a few moments they reached the broader trail without a mishap. A discussion regarding their future movements was already taking place. The impossibility of regaining the station at the Summit was admitted; the way down the mountain to the next settlement was still left to them, or the adjacent woods, if they wished for an encampment. The ostler once more assumed authority.

"'Skuse me, gentlemen, but them horses don't take no pasear down the mountain to-night. The stage-road ain't a mile off, and I kalkilate to wait here till the up stage comes. She's bound to stop on account of the snow; and I've done my dooty when I hand the horses over to the driver."

"But if she hears of the block up yer, and waits at the lower station?" said Rawlins.

"Then I've done my dooty all the same. 'Skuse me, gentlemen, but them ez hez their own horses kin do ez they like."

As this clearly pointed to Hale, he briefly assured his companions that he had no intention of deserting them. "If I cannot reach Eagle's Court, I shall at least keep as near it as possible. I suppose any messenger from my house to the Summit will learn where I am and why I am delayed?"

"Messenger from your house!" gasped Rawlins. "Are you crazy, stranger? Only a bird would get outer Eagle's now; and it would hev to be an eagle at that! Between your house and the Summit the snow must be ten feet by this time, to say nothing of the drift in the pass."

Hale felt it was the truth. At any other time he would have worried over this unexpected situation, and utter violation of all his traditions. He was past that now, and even felt a certain relief. He knew his family were safe; it was enough. That they were locked up securely, and incapable of interfering with HIM, seemed to enhance his new, half-conscious, half-shy enjoyment of an adventurous existence.

The ostler, who had been apparently lost in contemplation of the steep trail he had just descended, suddenly clapped his hand to his leg with an ejaculation of gratified astonishment.

"Waal, darn my skin ef that ain't Hennicker's 'slide' all the time! I heard it was somewhat about here."

Rawlins briefly explained to Hale that a slide was a rude incline for the transit of heavy goods that could not be carried down a trail.

"And Hennicker's," continued the man, "ain't more nor a mile away. Ye might try Hennicker's at a push, eh?"

By a common instinct the whole party looked dubiously at Hale. "Who's Hennicker?" he felt compelled to ask.

The ostler hesitated, and glanced at the others to reply. "There ARE folks," he said lazily, at last, "ez beleeves that Hennicker ain't much better nor the crowd we're hunting; but they don't say it TO Hennicker. We needn't let on what we're after."

"I for one," said Hale stoutly, "decidedly object to any concealment of our purpose."

"It don't follow," said Rawlins carelessly, "that Hennicker even knows of this yer robbery. It's his gineral gait we refer to. Ef yer think it more polite, and it makes it more sociable to discuss this matter afore him, I'm agreed."

"Hale means," said Clinch, "that it wouldn't be on the square to take and make use of any points we might pick up there agin the road agents."

"Certainly," said Hale. It was not at all what he had meant, but he felt singularly relieved at the compromise.

"And ez I reckon Hennicker ain't such a fool ez not to know who we are and what we're out for," continued Clinch, "I reckon there ain't any concealment."

"Then it's Hennicker's?" said the ostler, with swift deduction.

"Hennicker's it is! Lead on."

The ostler remounted his horse, and the others followed. The trail presently turned into a broader track, that bore some signs of approaching habitations, and at the end of five minutes they came upon a clearing. It was part of one of the fragmentary mountain terraces, and formed by itself a vast niche, or bracketed shelf, in the hollow flank of the mountain that, to Hale's first glance, bore a rude resemblance to Eagle's Court. But there was neither meadow nor open field; the few acres of ground had been wrested from the forest by axe and fire, and unsightly stumps everywhere marked the rude and difficult attempts at cultivation. Two or three rough buildings of unplaned and unpainted boards, connected by rambling sheds, stood in the centre of the amphitheatre. Far from being protected by the encircling rampart, it seemed to be the selected arena for the combating elements. A whirlwind from the outer abyss continually filled this cave of AEolus with driving snow, which, however, melted as it fell, or was quickly whirled away again.

A few dogs barked and ran out to meet the cavalcade, but there was no other sign of any life disturbed or concerned at their approach.

"I reckon Hennicker ain't home, or he'd hev been on the lookout afore this," said the ostler, dismounting and rapping on the door.

After a silence, a female voice, unintelligibly to the others, apparently had some colloquy with the ostler, who returned to the party.

"Must go in through the kitchin—can't open the door for the wind."

Leaving their horses in the shed, they entered the kitchen, which communicated, and presently came upon a square room filled with smoke from a fire of green pine logs. The doors and windows were tightly fastened; the only air came in through the large-throated chimney in voluminous gusts, which seemed to make the hollow shell of the apartment swell and expand to the point of bursting. Despite the stinging of the resinous smoke, the temperature was grateful to the benumbed travellers. Several cushionless arm-chairs, such as were used in bar-rooms, two tables, a sideboard, half bar and half cupboard, and a rocking-chair comprised the furniture, and a few bear and buffalo skins covered the floor. Hale sank into one of the arm-chairs, and, with a lazy satisfaction, partly born of his fatigue and partly from some newly-discovered appreciative faculty, gazed around the room, and then at the mistress of the house, with whom the others were talking.

She was tall, gaunt, and withered; in spite of her evident years, her twisted hair was still dark and full, and her eyes bright and piercing; her complexion and teeth had long since succumbed to the vitiating effects of frontier cookery, and her lips were stained with the yellow juice of a brier-wood pipe she held in her mouth. The ostler had explained their intrusion, and veiled their character under the vague epithet of a "hunting party," and was now evidently describing them personally. In his new-found philosophy the fact that the interest of his hostess seemed to be excited only by the names of his companions, that he himself was carelessly, and even deprecatingly, alluded to as the "stranger from Eagle's" by the ostler, and completely overlooked by the old woman, gave him no concern.

"You'll have to talk to Zenobia yourself. Dod rot ef I'm gine to interfere. She knows Hennicker's ways, and if she chooses to take in transients it ain't no funeral o' mine. Zeenie! You, Zeenie! Look yer!"

A tall, lazy-looking, handsome girl appeared on the threshold of the next room, and with a hand on each door-post slowly swung herself backwards and forwards, without entering. "Well, Maw?"

The old woman briefly and unalluringly pictured the condition of the travellers.

"Paw ain't here," began the girl doubtfully, "and—How dy, Dick! is that you?" The interruption was caused by her recognition of the ostler, and she lounged into the room. In spite of a skimp, slatternly gown, whose straight skirt clung to her lower limbs, there was a quaint, nymph-like contour to her figure. Whether from languor, ill-health, or more probably from a morbid consciousness of her own height, she moved with a slightly affected stoop that had become a habit. It did not seem ungraceful to Hale, already attracted by her delicate profile, her large dark eyes, and a certain weird resemblance she had to some half-domesticated dryad.

"That'll do, Maw," she said, dismissing her parent with a nod. "I'll talk to Dick."

As the door closed on the old woman, Zenobia leaned her hands on the back of a chair, and confronted the admiring eyes of Dick with a goddess-like indifference.

"Now wot's the use of your playin' this yer game on me, Dick? Wot's the good of your ladlin' out that hogwash about huntin'? HUNTIN'! I'll tell yer the huntin' you-uns hev been at! You've been huntin' George Lee and his boys since an hour before sun up. You've been followin' a blind trail up to the Ridge, until the snow got up and hunted YOU right here! You've been whoopin' and yellin' and circus-ridin' on the roads like ez yer wos Comanches, and frightening all the women folk within miles—that's your huntin'! You've been climbin' down Paw's old slide at last, and makin' tracks for here to save the skins of them condemned government horses of the Kempany! And THAT'S your huntin'!"

To Hale's surprise, a burst of laughter from the party followed this speech. He tried to join in, but this ridiculous summary of the result of his enthusiastic sense of duty left him—the only earnest believer mortified and embarrassed. Nor was he the less concerned as he found the girl's dark eyes had rested once or twice upon him curiously. Zenobia laughed too, and, lazily turning the chair around, dropped into it. "And by this time George Lee's loungin' back in his chyar and smokin' his cigyar somewhar in Sacramento," she added, stretching her feet out to the fire, and suiting the action to the word with an imaginary cigar between the long fingers of a thin and not over-clean hand.

"We cave, Zeenie!" said Rawlins, when their hilarity had subsided to a more subdued and scarcely less flattering admiration of the unconcerned goddess before them. "That's about the size of it. You kin rake down the pile. I forgot you're an old friend of George's."

"He's a white man!" said the girl decidedly.

"Ye used to know him?" continued Rawlins.

"Once. Paw ain't in that line now," she said simply.

There was such a sublime unconsciousness of any moral degradation involved in this allusion that even Hale accepted it without a shock. She rose presently, and, going to the little sideboard, brought out a number of glasses; these she handed to each of the party, and then, producing a demijohn of whiskey, slung it dexterously and gracefully over her arm, so that it rested on her elbow like a cradle, and, going to each one in succession, filled their glasses. It obliged each one to rise to accept the libation, and as Hale did so in his turn he met the dark eyes of the girl full on his own. There was a pleased curiosity in her glance that made this married man of thirty-five color as awkwardly as a boy.

The tender of refreshment being understood as a tacit recognition of their claims to a larger hospitality, all further restraint was removed. Zenobia resumed her seat, and placing her elbow on the arm of her chair, and her small round chin in her hand, looked thoughtfully in the fire. "When I say George Lee's a white man, it ain't because I know him. It's his general gait. Wot's he ever done that's underhanded or mean? Nothin'! You kant show the poor man he's ever took a picayune from. When he's helped himself to a pile it's been outer them banks or them express companies, that think it mighty fine to bust up themselves, and swindle the poor folks o' their last cent, and nobody talks o' huntin' THEM! And does he keep their money? No; he passes it round among the boys that help him, and they put it in circulation. HE don't keep it for himself; he ain't got fine houses in Frisco; he don't keep fast horses for show. Like ez not the critter he did that job with—ef it was him—none of you boys would have rid! And he takes all the risks himself; you ken bet your life that every man with him was safe and away afore he turned his back on you-uns."

"He certainly drops a little of his money at draw poker, Zeenie," said Clinch, laughing. "He lost five thousand dollars to Sheriff Kelly last week."

"Well, I don't hear of the sheriff huntin' him to give it back, nor do I reckon Kelly handed it over to the Express it was taken from. I heard YOU won suthin' from him a spell ago. I reckon you've been huntin' him to find out whar you should return it." The laugh was clearly against Clinch. He was about to make some rallying rejoinder when the young girl suddenly interrupted him. "Ef you're wantin' to hunt somebody, why don't you take higher game? Thar's that Jim Harkins: go for him, and I'll join you."

"Harkins!" exclaimed Clinch and Hale simultaneously.

"Yes, Jim Harkins; do you know him?" she said, glancing from one to the other.

"One of my friends do," said Clinch laughing; "but don't let that stop you."

"And YOU—over there," continued Zenobia, bending her head and eyes towards Hale.

"The fact is—I believe he was my banker," said Hale, with a smile. "I don't know him personally."

"Then you'd better hunt him before he does you."

"What's HE done, Zeenie?" asked Rawlins, keenly enjoying the discomfiture of the others.

"What?" She stopped, threw her long black braids over her shoulder, clasped her knee with her hands, and rocking backwards and forwards, sublimely unconscious of the apparition of a slim ankle and half-dropped-off slipper from under her shortened gown, continued, "It mightn't please HIM," she said slyly, nodding towards Hale.

"Pray don't mind me," said Hale, with unnecessary eagerness.

"Well," said Zenobia, "I reckon you all know Ned Falkner and the Excelsior Ditch?"

"Yes, Falkner's the superintendent of it," said Rawlins. "And a square man too. Thar ain't anything mean about him."

"Shake," said Zenobia, extending her hand. Rawlins shook the proffered hand with eager spontaneousness, and the girl resumed: "He's about ez good ez they make 'em—you bet. Well, you know Ned has put all his money, and all his strength, and all his sabe, and—"

"His good looks," added Clinch mischievously.

"Into that Ditch," continued Zenobia, ignoring the interruption. "It's his mother, it's his sweetheart, it's his everything! When other chaps of his age was cavortin' round Frisco, and havin' high jinks, Ned was in his Ditch. 'Wait till the Ditch is done,' he used to say. 'Wait till she begins to boom, and then you just stand round.' Mor'n that, he got all the boys to put in their last cent—for they loved Ned, and love him now, like ez ef he wos a woman."

"That's so," said Clinch and Rawlins simultaneously, "and he's worth it."

"Well," continued Zenobia, "the Ditch didn't boom ez soon ez they kalkilated. And then the boys kept gettin' poorer and poorer, and Ned he kept gettin' poorer and poorer in everything but his hopefulness and grit. Then he looks around for more capital. And about this time, that coyote Harkins smelt suthin' nice up there, and he gits Ned to give him control of it, and he'll lend him his name and fix up a company. Soon ez he gets control, the first thing he does is to say that it wants half a million o' money to make it pay, and levies an assessment of two hundred dollars a share. That's nothin' for them rich fellows to pay, or pretend to pay, but for boys on grub wages it meant only ruin. They couldn't pay, and had to forfeit their shares for next to nothing. And Ned made one more desperate attempt to save them and himself by borrowing money on his shares; when that hound Harkins got wind of it, and let it be buzzed around that the Ditch is a failure, and that he was goin' out of it; that brought the shares down to nothing. As Ned couldn't raise a dollar, the new company swooped down on his shares for the debts THEY had put up, and left him and the boys to help themselves. Ned couldn't bear to face the boys that he'd helped to ruin, and put out, and ain't been heard from since. After Harkins had got rid of Ned and the boys he manages to pay off that wonderful debt, and sells out for a hundred thousand dollars. That money—Ned's money—he sends to Sacramento, for he don't dare to travel with it himself, and is kalkilatin' to leave the kentry, for some of the boys allow to kill him on sight. So ef you're wantin' to hunt suthin', thar's yer chance, and you needn't go inter the snow to do it."

"But surely the law can recover this money?" said Hale indignantly. "It is as infamous a robbery as—" He stopped as he caught Zenobia's eye.

"Ez last night's, you were goin' to say. I'll call it MORE. Them road agents don't pretend to be your friend—but take yer money and run their risks. For ez to the law—that can't help yer."

"It's a skin game, and you might ez well expect to recover a gambling debt from a short-card sharp," explained Clinch; "Falkner oughter shot him on sight."

"Or the boys lynched him," suggested Rawlins.

"I think," said Hale, more reflectively, "that in the absence of legal remedy a man of that kind should have been forced under strong physical menace to give up his ill-gotten gains. The money was the primary object, and if that could be got without bloodshed—which seems to me a useless crime—it would be quite as effective. Of course, if there was resistance or retaliation, it might be necessary to kill him."

He had unconsciously fallen into his old didactic and dogmatic habit of speech, and perhaps, under the spur of Zenobia's eyes, he had given it some natural emphasis. A dead silence followed, in which the others regarded him with amused and gratified surprise, and it was broken only by Zenobia rising and holding out her hand. "Shake!"

Hale raised it gallantly, and pressed his lips on the one spotless finger.

"That's gospel truth. And you ain't the first white man to say it."

"Indeed," laughed Hale. "Who was the other?"

"George Lee!"

CHAPTER VI

The laughter that followed was interrupted by a sudden barking of the dogs in the outer clearing. Zenobia rose lazily and strode to the window. It relieved Hale of certain embarrassing reflections suggested by her comment.

"Ef it ain't that God-forsaken fool Dick bringing up passengers from the snow-bound up stage in the road! I reckon I'VE got suthin' to say to that!" But the later appearance of the apologetic Dick, with the assurance that the party carried a permission from her father, granted at the lower station in view of such an emergency, checked her active opposition. "That's like Paw," she soliloquized aggrievedly; "shuttin' us up and settin' dogs on everybody for a week, and then lettin' the whole stage service pass through one door and out at another. Well, it's HIS house and HIS whiskey, and they kin take it, but they don't get me to help 'em."

They certainly were not a prepossessing or good-natured acquisition to the party. Apart from the natural antagonism which, on such occasions, those in possession always feel towards the new-comer, they were strongly inclined to resist the dissatisfied querulousness and aggressive attitude of these fresh applicants for hospitality. The most offensive one was a person who appeared to exercise some authority over the others. He was loud, assuming, and dressed with vulgar pretension. He quickly disposed himself in the chair vacated by Zenobia, and called for some liquor.

"I reckon you'll hev to help yourself," said Rawlins dryly, as the summons met with no response. "There are only two women in the house, and I reckon their hands are full already."

"I call it d—d uncivil treatment," said the man, raising his voice; "and Hennicker had better sing smaller if he don't want his old den pulled down some day. He ain't any better than men that hev been picked up afore now."

"You oughter told him that, and mebbe he'd hev come over with yer," returned Rawlins. "He's a mild, soft, easy-going man, is Hennicker! Ain't he, Colonel Clinch?"

The casual mention of Clinch's name produced the effect which the speaker probably intended. The stranger stared at Clinch, who, apparently oblivious of the conversation, was blinking his cold gray eyes at the fire. Dropping his aggressive tone to mere querulousness, the man sought the whiskey demijohn, and helped himself and his companions. Fortified by liquor he returned to the fire.

"I reckon you've heard about this yer robbery, Colonel," he said, addressing Clinch, with an attempt at easy familiarity.

Without raising his eyes from the fire, Clinch briefly assented, "I reckon."

"I'm up yer, examining into it, for the Express."

"Lost much?" asked Rawlins.

"Not so much ez they might hev. That fool Harkins had a hundred thousand dollars in greenbacks sealed up like an ordinary package of a thousand dollars, and gave it to a friend, Bill Guthrie, in the bank to pick out some unlikely chap among the passengers to take charge of it to Reno. He wouldn't trust the Express. Ha! ha!"

The dead, oppressive silence that followed his empty laughter made it seem almost artificial. Rawlins held his breath and looked at Clinch. Hale, with the instincts of a refined, sensitive man, turned hot with the embarrassment Clinch should have shown. For that gentleman, without lifting his eyes from the fire, and with no apparent change in his demeanor, lazily asked—

"Ye didn't ketch the name o' that passenger?"

"Naturally, no! For when Guthrie heard what was said agin him he wouldn't give his name until he heard from him."

"And WHAT was said agin him?" asked Clinch musingly.

"What would be said agin a man that give up that sum o' money, like a chaw of tobacco, for the asking? Why, there were but three men, as far ez we kin hear, that did the job. And there were four passengers inside, armed, and the driver and express messenger on the box. Six were robbed by THREE!—they were a sweet-scented lot! Reckon they must hev felt mighty small, for I hear they got up and skedaddled from the station under the pretext of lookin' for the robbers." He laughed again, and the laugh was noisily repeated by his five companions at the other end of the room.

Hale, who had forgotten that the stranger was only echoing a part of his own criticism of eight hours before, was on the point of rising with burning cheeks and angry indignation, when the lazily uplifted eye of Clinch caught his, and absolutely held him down with its paralyzing and deadly significance. Murder itself seemed to look from those cruelly quiet and remorseless gray pupils. For a moment he forgot his own rage in this glimpse of Clinch's implacable resentment; for a moment he felt a thrill of pity for the wretch who had provoked it. He remained motionless and fascinated in his chair as the lazy lids closed like a sheath over Clinch's eyes again. Rawlins, who had probably received the same glance of warning, remained equally still.

"They haven't heard the last of it yet, you bet," continued the infatuated stranger. "I've got a little statement here for the newspaper," he added, drawing some papers from his pocket; "suthin' I just run off in the coach as I came along. I reckon it'll show things up in a new light. It's time there should be some change. All the cussin' that's been usually done hez been by the passengers agin the express and stage companies. I propose that the Company should do a little cussin' themselves. See? P'r'aps you don't mind my readin' it to ye? It's just spicy enough to suit them newspaper chaps."

"Go on," said Colonel Clinch quietly.

The man cleared his throat, with the preliminary pose of authorship, and his five friends, to whom the composition was evidently not unfamiliar, assumed anticipatory smiles.

"I call it 'Prize Pusillanimous Passengers.' Sort of runs easy off the tongue, you know.

"'It now appears that the success of the late stagecoach robbery near the Summit was largely due to the pusillanimity —not to use a more serious word'"—He stopped, and looked explanatorily towards Clinch: "Ye'll see in a minit what I'm gettin' at by that pusillanimity of the passengers themselves.

'It now transpires that there were only three robbers who attacked the coach, and that although passengers, driver, and express messenger were fully armed, and were double the number of their assailants, not a shot was fired. We mean no reflections upon the well-known courage of Yuba Bill, nor the experience and coolness of Bracy Tibbetts, the courteous express messenger, both of whom have since confessed to have been more than astonished at the Christian and lamb-like submission of the insiders. Amusing stories of some laughable yet sickening incidents of the occasion—such as grown men kneeling in the road, and offering to strip themselves completely, if their lives were only spared; of one of the passengers hiding under the seat, and only being dislodged by pulling his coat-tails; of incredible sums promised, and even offers of menial service, for the preservation of their wretched carcases—are received with the greatest gusto; but we are in possession of facts which may lead to more serious accusations. Although one of the passengers is said to have lost a large sum of money intrusted to him, while attempting with barefaced effrontery to establish a rival "carrying" business in one of the Express Company's own coaches—'I call that a good point." He interrupted himself to allow the unrestrained applause of his own party. "Don't you?"

"It's just h-ll," said Clinch musingly.

"'Yet the affair," resumed the stranger from his manuscript, "'is locked up in great and suspicious mystery. The presence of Jackson N. Stanner, Esq.' (that's me), 'special detective agent to the Company, and his staff in town, is a guaranty that the mystery will be thoroughly probed.' Hed to put that in to please the Company," he again deprecatingly explained. "'We are indebted to this gentleman for the facts.'"

"The pint you want to make in that article," said Clinch,

rising, but still directing his face and his conversation to the fire, "ez far ez I ken see ez that no three men kin back down six unless they be cowards, or are willing to be backed down."

"That's the point what I start from," rejoined Stanner, "and work up. I leave it to you ef it ain't so."

"I can't say ez I agree with you," said the Colonel dryly. He turned, and still without lifting his eyes walked towards the door of the room which Zenobia had entered. The key was on the inside, but Clinch gently opened the door, removed the key, and closing the door again locked it from his side. Hale and Rawlins felt their hearts beat quickly; the others followed Clinch's slow movements and downcast mien with amused curiosity. After locking the other outlet from the room, and putting the keys in his pocket, Clinch returned to the fire. For the first time he lifted his eyes; the man nearest him shrank back in terror.

"I am the man," he said slowly, taking deliberate breath between his sentences, "who gave up those greenbacks to the robbers. I am one of the three passengers you have lampooned in that paper, and these gentlemen beside me are the other two." He stopped and looked around him. "You don't believe that three men can back down six! Well, I'll show you how it can be done. More than that, I'll show you how ONE man can do it; for, by the living G-d, if you don't hand over that paper I'll kill you where you sit! I'll give you until I count ten; if one of you moves he and you are dead men—but YOU first!"

Before he had finished speaking Hale and Rawlins had both risen, as if in concert, with their weapons drawn. Hale could not tell how or why he had done so, but he was equally conscious, without knowing why, of fixing his eye on one of the other party, and that he should, in the event of an affray, try to kill him. He did not attempt to reason; he only knew that he should do his best to kill that man and perhaps others.

"One," said Clinch, lifting his derringer, "two—three—"

"Look here, Colonel—I swear I didn't know it was you. Come—d—m it! I say—see here," stammered Stanner, with white cheeks, not daring to glance for aid to his stupefied party.

"Four—five—six—"

"Wait! Here!" He produced the paper and threw it on the floor.

"Pick it up and hand it to me. Seven—eight—"

Stanner hastily scrambled to his feet, picked up the paper, and handed it to the Colonel. "I was only joking, Colonel," he said, with a forced laugh.

"I'm glad to hear it. But as this joke is in black and white, you wouldn't mind saying so in the same fashion. Take that pen and ink and write as I dictate. 'I certify that I am satisfied that the above statement is a base calumny against the characters of Ringwood Clinch, Robert Rawlins, and John Hale, passengers, and that I do hereby apologize to the same.' Sign it. That'll do. Now let the rest of your party sign as witnesses."

They complied without hesitation; some, seizing the opportunity of treating the affair as a joke, suggested a drink.

"Excuse me," said Clinch quietly, "but ez this house ain't big enough for me and that man, and ez I've got business at Wild

Cat Station with this paper, I think I'll go without drinkin'."
He took the keys from his pocket, unlocked the doors, and
taking up his overcoat and rifle turned as if to go.

Rawlins rose to follow him; Hale alone hesitated. The rapid
occurrences of the last half hour gave him no time for
reflection. But he was by no means satisfied of the legality of
the last act he had aided and abetted, although he admitted its
rude justice, and felt he would have done so again. A fear of
this, and an instinct that he might be led into further
complications if he continued to identify himself with Clinch
and Rawlins; the fact that they had professedly abandoned
their quest, and that it was really supplanted by the presence
of an authorized party whom they had already come in
conflict with—all this urged him to remain behind. On the
other hand, the apparent desertion of his comrades at the last
moment was opposed both to his sense of honor and the
liking he had taken to them. But he reflected that he had
already shown his active partisanship, that he could be of
little service to them at Wild Cat Station, and would be only
increasing the distance from his home; and above all, an
impatient longing for independent action finally decided
him. "I think I'll stay here," he said to Clinch, "unless you
want me."

Clinch cast a swift and meaning glance at the enemy, but
looked approval. "Keep your eyes skinned, and you're good
for a dozen of 'em," he said sotto voce, and then turned to
Stanner. "I'm going to take this paper to Wild Cat. If you
want to communicate with me hereafter you know where I
am to be found, unless"—he smiled grimly—"you'd like to
see me outside for a few minutes before I go?"

"It is a matter that concerns the Stage Company, not me,"
said Stanner, with an attempt to appear at his ease.

Hale accompanied Clinch and Rawlins through the kitchen to the stables. The ostler, Dick, had already returned to the rescue of the snow-bound coach.

"I shouldn't like to leave many men alone with that crowd," said Clinch, pressing Hale's hand; "and I wouldn't have allowed your staying behind ef I didn't know I could bet my pile on you. Your offerin' to stay just puts a clean finish on it. Look yer, Hale, I didn't cotton much to you at first; but ef you ever want a friend, call on Ringwood Clinch."

"The same here, old man," said Rawlins, extending his hand as he appeared from a hurried conference with the old woman at the woodshed, "and trust to Zeenie to give you a hint ef there's anythin' underhanded goin' on. So long."

Half inclined to resent this implied suggestion of protection, yet half pleased at the idea of a confidence with the handsome girl he had seen, Hale returned to the room. A whispered discussion among the party ceased on his entering, and an awkward silence followed, which Hale did not attempt to break as he quietly took his seat again by the fire. He was presently confronted by Stanner, who with an affectation of easy familiarity crossed over to the hearth.

"The old Kernel's d—d peppery and high toned when he's got a little more than his reg'lar three fingers o' corn juice, eh?"

"I must beg you to understand distinctly, Mr. Stanner," said Hale, with a return of his habitual precision of statement, "that I regard any slighting allusion to the gentleman who has just left not only as in exceedingly bad taste coming from YOU, but very offensive to myself. If you mean to imply that he was under the influence of liquor, it is my duty to undeceive you; he was so perfectly in possession of his faculties as to express not only his own but MY opinion of your conduct. You must also admit that he was discriminating enough to show his objection to your company by leaving it. I regret that circumstances do not make it convenient for me to exercise that privilege; but if I am obliged to put up with your presence in this room, I strongly insist that it is not made unendurable with the addition of your conversation."

The effect of this deliberate and passionless declaration was more discomposing to the party than Clinch's fury. Utterly unaccustomed to the ideas and language suddenly confronting them, they were unable to determine whether it was the real expression of the speaker, or whether it was a vague badinage or affectation to which any reply would involve them in ridicule. In a country terrorized by practical joking, they did not doubt but that this was a new form of hoaxing calculated to provoke some response that would constitute them as victims. The immediate effect upon them was that complete silence in regard to himself that Hale desired. They drew together again and conversed in whispers, while Hale, with his eyes fixed on the fire, gave himself up to somewhat late and useless reflection.

He could scarcely realize his position. For however he might look at it, within a space of twelve hours he had not only changed some of his most cherished opinions, but he had acted in accordance with that change in a way that made it seem almost impossible for him ever to recant. In the interests of law and order he had engaged in an unlawful and disorderly pursuit of criminals, and had actually come in conflict not with the criminals, but with the only party apparently authorized to pursue them. More than that, he was finding himself committed to a certain sympathy with the criminals. Twenty-four hours ago, if anyone had told him that he would have condoned an illegal act for its abstract justice, or assisted to commit an illegal act for the same purpose, he would have felt himself insulted. That he knew he would not now feel it as an insult perplexed him still more. In these circumstances the fact that he was separated from his family, and as it were from all his past life and traditions, by a chance accident, did not disturb him greatly; indeed, he was for the first time a little doubtful of their probable criticism on his inconsistency, and was by no means in a hurry to subject himself to it.

Lifting his eyes, he was suddenly aware that the door leading to the kitchen was slowly opening. He had thought he heard it creak once or twice during his deliberate reply to Stanner. It was evidently moving now so as to attract his attention, without disturbing the others. It presently opened sufficiently wide to show the face of Zeenie, who, with a gesture of caution towards his companions, beckoned him to join her. He rose carelessly as if going out, and, putting on his hat, entered the kitchen as the retreating figure of the young girl glided lightly towards the stables. She ascended a few open steps as if to a hay-loft, but stopped before a low door. Pushing it open, she preceded him into a small room, apparently under the roof, which scarcely allowed her to stand upright. By the light of a stable lantern hanging from a beam he saw that, though poorly furnished, it bore some evidence of feminine taste and habitation. Motioning to the only chair, she seated herself on the edge of the bed, with her hands clasping her knees in her familiar attitude. Her face bore traces of recent agitation, and her eyes were shining with tears. By the closer light of the lantern he was surprised to find it was from laughter.

"I reckoned you'd be right lonely down there with that Stanner crowd, particklerly after that little speech o' your'n, so I sez to Maw I'd get you up yer for a spell. Maw and I heerd you exhort 'em! Maw allowed you woz talkin' a furrin' tongue all along, but I—sakes alive!—I hed to hump myself to keep from bustin' into a yell when yer jist drawed them Webster-unabridged sentences on 'em." She stopped and rocked backwards and forwards with a laugh that, subdued by the proximity of the roof and the fear of being overheard, was by no means unmusical. "I'll tell ye whot got me, though! That part commencing, 'Suckamstances over which I've no controul.'"

"Oh, come! I didn't say that," interrupted Hale, laughing.

"'Don't make it convenient for me to exercise the privilege of kickin' yer out to that extent,'" she continued; "'but if I cannot dispense with your room, the least I can say is that it's a d—d sight better than your company—'or suthin' like that! And then the way you minded your stops, and let your voice rise and fall just ez easy ez if you wos a First Reader in large type. Why, the Kernel wasn't nowhere. HIS cussin' didn't come within a mile o' yourn. That Stanner jist turned yaller."

"I'm afraid you are laughing at me," said Hale, not knowing whether to be pleased or vexed at the girl's amusement.

"I reckon I'm the only one that dare do it, then," said the girl simply. "The Kernel sez the way you turned round after he'd done his cussin', and said yer believed you'd stay and take the responsibility of the whole thing—and did, in that kam, soft, did-anybody-speak-to-me style—was the neatest thing he'd seen yet. No! Maw says I ain't much on manners, but I know a man when I see him."

For an instant Hale gave himself up to the delicious flattery of unexpected, unintended, and apparently uninterested compliment. Becoming at last a little embarrassed under the frank curiosity of the girl's dark eyes, he changed the subject.

"Do you always come up here through the stables?" he asked, glancing round the room, which was evidently her own.

"I reckon," she answered half abstractedly. "There's a ladder down thar to Maw's room"—pointing to a trapdoor beside the broad chimney that served as a wall—"but it's handier the other way, and nearer the bosses if you want to get away quick."

This palpable suggestion—borne out by what he remembered of the other domestic details—that the house had been planned with reference to sudden foray or escape reawakened his former uneasy reflections. Zeenie, who had been watching his face, added, "It's no slouch, when b'ar or painters hang round nights and stampede the stock, to be able to swing yourself on to a boss whenever you hear a row going on outside."

"Do you mean that YOU—"

"Paw USED, and I do NOW, sense I've come into the room." She pointed to a nondescript garment, half cloak, half habit, hanging on the wall. "I've been outer bed and on Pitchpine's back as far ez the trail five minutes arter I heard the first bellow."

Hale regarded her with undisguised astonishment. There was nothing at all Amazonian or horsey in her manners, nor was there even the robust physical contour that might have been developed through such experiences. On the contrary, she seemed to be lazily effeminate in body and mind. Heedless of his critical survey of her, she beckoned him to draw his chair nearer, and, looking into his eyes, said—

"Whatever possessed YOU to take to huntin' men?"

Hale was staggered by the question, but nevertheless endeavored to explain. But he was surprised to find that his explanation appeared stilted even to himself, and, he could not doubt, was utterly incomprehensible to the girl. She nodded her head, however, and continued—

"Then you haven't anythin' agin' George?"

"I don't know George," said Hale, smiling. "My proceeding was against the highwayman."

"Well, HE was the highwayman."

"I mean, it was the principle I objected to—a principle that I consider highly dangerous."

"Well HE is the principal, for the others only HELPED, I reckon," said Zeenie with a sigh, "and I reckon he IS dangerous."

Hale saw it was useless to explain. The girl continued—

"What made you stay here instead of going on with the Kernel? There was suthin' else besides your wanting to make that Stanner take water. What is it?"

A light sense of the propinquity of beauty, of her confidence, of their isolation, of the eloquence of her dark eyes, at first tempted Hale to a reply of simple gallantry; a graver consideration of the same circumstances froze it upon his lips.

"I don't know," he returned awkwardly.

"Well, I'll tell you," she said. "You didn't cotton to the Kernel and Rawlins much more than you did to Stanner.

They ain't your kind."

In his embarrassment Hale blundered upon the thought he had honorably avoided.

"Suppose," he said, with a constrained laugh, "I had stayed to see you."

"I reckon I ain't your kind, neither," she replied promptly. There was a momentary pause when she rose and walked to the chimney. "It's very quiet down there," she said, stooping and listening over the roughly-boarded floor that formed the ceiling of the room below. "I wonder what's going on."

In the belief that this was a delicate hint for his return to the party he had left, Hale rose, but the girl passed him hurriedly, and, opening the door, cast a quick glance into the stable beyond.

"Just as I reckoned—the horses are gone too. They've skedaddled," she said blankly.

Hale did not reply. In his embarrassment a moment ago the idea of taking an equally sudden departure had flashed upon him. Should he take this as a justification of that impulse, or how? He stood irresolutely gazing at the girl, who turned and began to descend the stairs silently. He followed. When they reached the lower room they found it as they had expected—deserted.

"I hope I didn't drive them away," said Hale, with an uneasy look at the troubled face of the girl. "For I really had an idea of going myself a moment ago."

She remained silent, gazing out of the window. Then, turning with a slight shrug of her shoulders, said half defiantly:

"What's the use now? Oh, Maw! the Stanner crowd has vamosed the ranch, and this yer stranger kalkilates to stay!"

CHAPTER VII

A week had passed at Eagle's Court—a week of mingled clouds and sunshine by day, of rain over the green plateau and snow on the mountain by night. Each morning had brought its fresh greenness to the winter-girt domain, and a fresh coat of dazzling white to the barrier that separated its dwellers from the world beyond. There was little change in the encompassing wall of their prison; if anything, the snowy circle round them seemed to have drawn its lines nearer day by day. The immediate result of this restricted limit had been to confine the range of cattle to the meadows nearer the house, and at a safe distance from the fringe of wilderness now invaded by the prowling tread of predatory animals.

Nevertheless, the two figures lounging on the slope at sunset gave very little indication of any serious quality in the situation. Indeed, so far as appearances were concerned, Kate, who was returning from an afternoon stroll with Falkner, exhibited, with feminine inconsistency, a decided return to the world of fashion and conventionality apparently just as she was effectually excluded from it. She had not only discarded her white dress as a concession to the practical evidence of the surrounding winter, but she had also brought out a feather hat and sable muff which had once graced a fashionable suburb of Boston. Even Falkner had exchanged his slouch hat and picturesque serape for a beaver overcoat

Bret Harte

and fur cap of Hale's which had been pressed upon him by Kate, under the excuse of the exigencies of the season. Within a stone's throw of the thicket, turbulent with the savage forces of nature, they walked with the abstraction of people hearing only their own voices; in the face of the solemn peaks clothed with white austerity they talked gravely of dress.

"I don't mean to say," said Kate demurely, "that you're to give up the serape entirely; you can wear it on rainy nights and when you ride over here from your friend's house to spend the evening—for the sake of old times," she added, with an unconscious air of referring to an already antiquated friendship; "but you must admit it's a little too gorgeous and theatrical for the sunlight of day and the public highway."

"But why should that make it wrong, if the experience of a people has shown it to be a garment best fitted for their wants and requirements?" said Falkner argumentatively.

"But you are not one of those people," said Kate, "and that makes all the difference. You look differently and act differently, so that there is something irreconcilable between your clothes and you that makes you look odd."

"And to look odd, according to your civilized prejudices, is to be wrong," said Falkner bitterly.

"It is to seem different from what one really is—which IS wrong. Now, you are a mining superintendent, you tell me. Then you don't want to look like a Spanish brigand, as you do in that serape. I am sure if you had ridden up to a stage-coach while I was in it, I'd have handed you my watch and purse without a word. There! you are not offended?" she added, with a laugh, which did not, however, conceal a certain earnestness. "I suppose I ought to have said I would have given it gladly to such a romantic figure, and perhaps have got out and danced a saraband or bolero with you—if that is the thing to do nowadays. Well!" she said, after a dangerous pause, "consider that I've said it."

He had been walking a little before her, with his face turned towards the distant mountain. Suddenly he stopped and faced her. "You would have given enough of your time to the highwayman, Miss Scott, as would have enabled you to identify him for the police—and no more. Like your brother, you would have been willing to sacrifice yourself for the benefit of the laws of civilization and good order."

If a denial to this assertion could have been expressed without the use of speech, it was certainly transparent in the face and eyes of the young girl at that moment. If Falkner had been less self-conscious he would have seen it plainly. But Kate only buried her face in her lifted muff, slightly raised her pretty shoulders, and, dropping her tremulous eyelids, walked on. "It seems a pity," she said, after a pause, "that we cannot preserve our own miserable existence without taking something from others—sometimes even a life!" He started. "And it's horrid to have to remind you that you have yet to kill something for the invalid's supper," she continued. "I saw a hare in the field yonder."

"You mean that jackass rabbit?" he said, abstractedly.

"What you please. It's a pity you didn't take your gun instead of your rifle."

"I brought the rifle for protection."

"And a shot gun is only aggressive, I suppose?"

Falkner looked at her for a moment, and then, as the hare

suddenly started across the open a hundred yards away, brought the rifle to his shoulder. A long interval—as it seemed to Kate—elapsed; the animal appeared to be already safely out of range, when the rifle suddenly cracked; the hare bounded in the air like a ball, and dropped motionless. The girl looked at the marksman in undisguised admiration. "Is it quite dead?" she said timidly.

"It never knew what struck it."

"It certainly looks less brutal than shooting it with a shot gun, as John does, and then not killing it outright," said Kate. "I hate what is called sport and sportsmen, but a rifle seems—"

"What?" said Falkner.

"More—gentlemanly."

She had raised her pretty head in the air, and, with her hand shading her eyes, was looking around the clear ether, and said meditatively, "I wonder—no matter."

"What is it?"

"Oh, nothing."

"It is something," said Falkner, with an amused smile, reloading his rifle.

"Well, you once promised me an eagle's feather for my hat. Isn't that thing an eagle?"

"I am afraid it's only a hawk."

"Well, that will do. Shoot that!"

Her eyes were sparkling. Falkner withdrew his own with a slight smile, and raised his rifle with provoking deliberation.

"Are you quite sure it's what you want?" he asked demurely.

"Yes—quick!"

Nevertheless, it was some minutes before the rifle cracked again. The wheeling bird suddenly struck the wind with its wings aslant, and then fell like a plummet at a distance which showed the difficulty of the feat. Falkner started from her side before the bird reached the ground. He returned to her after a lapse of a few moments, bearing a trailing wing in his hand. "You shall make your choice," he said gayly.

"Are you sure it was killed outright?"

"Head shot off," said Falkner briefly.

"And besides, the fall would have killed it," said Kate conclusively. "It's lovely. I suppose they call you a very good shot?"

"They—who?"

"Oh! the people you know—your friends, and their sisters."

"George shoots better than I do, and has had more experience. I've seen him do that with a pistol. Of course not such a long shot, but a more difficult one."

Kate did not reply, but her face showed a conviction that as an artistic and gentlemanly performance it was probably inferior to the one she had witnessed. Falkner, who had picked up the hare also, again took his place by her side, as they turned towards the house.

"Do you remember the day you came, when we were walking here, you pointed out that rock on the mountain where the poor animals had taken refuge from the snow?" said Kate suddenly.

"Yes," answered Falkner; "they seem to have diminished. I am afraid you were right; they have either eaten each other or escaped. Let us hope the latter."

"I looked at them with a glass every day," said Kate, "and they've got down to only four. There's a bear and that shabby, over-grown cat you call a California lion, and a wolf, and a creature like a fox or a squirrel."

"It's a pity they're not all of a kind," said Falkner.

"Why?"

"There'd be nothing to keep them from being comfortable together."

"On the contrary, I should think it would be simply awful to be shut up entirely with one's own kind."

"Then you believe it is possible for them, with their different natures and habits, to be happy together?" said Falkner, with sudden earnestness.

"I believe," said Kate hurriedly, "that the bear and the lion find the fox and the wolf very amusing, and that the fox and the wolf—"

"Well?" said Falkner, stopping short.

"Well, the fox and the wolf will carry away a much better opinion of the lion and bear than they had before."

They had reached the house by this time, and for some occult reason Kate did not immediately enter the parlor, where she had left her sister and the invalid, who had already been promoted to a sofa and a cushion by the window, but proceeded directly to her own room. As a manoeuvre to avoid meeting Mrs. Hale, it was scarcely necessary, for that lady was already in advance of her on the staircase, as if she had left the parlor for a moment before they entered the house. Falkner, too, would have preferred the company of his own thoughts, but Lee, apparently the only unpreoccupied, all-pervading, and boyishly alert spirit in the party, hailed him from within, and obliged him to present himself on the threshold of the parlor with the hare and hawk's wing he was still carrying. Eying the latter with affected concern, Lee said gravely: "Of course, I CAN eat it, Ned, and I dare say it's the best part of the fowl, and the hare isn't more than enough for the women, but I had no idea we were so reduced. Three hours and a half gunning, and only one hare and a hawk's wing. It's terrible."

Perceiving that his friend was alone, Falkner dropped his burden in the hall and strode rapidly to his side. "Look here, George, we must, I must leave this place at once. It's no use talking; I can stand this sort of thing no longer."

"Nor can I, with the door open. Shut it, and say what you want quick, before Mrs. Hale comes back. Have you found a trail?"

"No, no; that's not what I mean."

"Well, it strikes me it ought to be, if you expect to get away. Have you proposed to Beacon Street, and she thinks it rather premature on a week's acquaintance?"

"No; but—"

"But you WILL, you mean? DON'T, just yet."

"But I cannot live this perpetual lie."

"That depends. I don't know HOW you're lying when I'm not with you. If you're walking round with that girl, singing hymns and talking of your class in Sunday-school, or if you're insinuating that you're a millionaire, and think of buying the place for a summer hotel, I should say you'd better quit that kind of lying. But, on the other hand, I don't see the necessity of your dancing round here with a shot gun, and yelling for Harkins's blood, or counting that package of greenbacks in the lap of Miss Scott, to be truthful. It seems to me there ought to be something between the two."

"But, George, don't you think—you are on such good terms with Mrs. Hale and her mother—that you might tell them the whole story? That is, tell it in your own way; they will hear anything from you, and believe it."

"Thank you; but suppose I don't believe in lying, either?"

"You know what I mean! You have a way, d—n it, of making everything seem like a matter of course, and the most natural thing going."

"Well, suppose I did. Are you prepared for the worst?"

Falkner was silent for a moment, and then replied, "Yes, anything would be better than this suspense."

"I don't agree with you. Then you would be willing to have them forgive us?"

"I don't understand you."

"I mean that their forgiveness would be the worst thing that could happen. Look here, Ned. Stop a moment; listen at that door. Mrs. Hale has the tread of an angel, with the pervading capacity of a cat. Now listen! I don't pretend to be in love with anybody here, but if I were I should hardly take advantage of a woman's helplessness and solitude with a sensational story about myself. It's not giving her a fair show. You know she won't turn you out of the house."

"No," said Falkner, reddening; "but I should expect to go at once, and that would be my only excuse for telling her."

"Go! where? In your preoccupation with that girl you haven't even found the trail by which Manuel escaped. Do you intend to camp outside the house, and make eyes at her when she comes to the window?"

"Because you think nothing of flirting with Mrs. Hale," said Falkner bitterly, "you care little—"

"My dear Ned," said Lee, "the fact that Mrs. Hale has a husband, and knows that she can't marry me, puts us on equal terms. Nothing that she could learn about me hereafter would make a flirtation with me any less wrong than it would be now, or make her seem more a victim. Can you say the same of yourself and that Puritan girl?"

"But you did not advise me to keep aloof from her; on the contrary, you—"

"I thought you might make the best of the situation, and pay her some attention, BECAUSE you could not go any further."

"You thought I was utterly heartless and selfish, like—"

Bret Harte

"Ned!"

Falkner walked rapidly to the fireplace, and returned.

"Forgive me, George—I'm a fool—and an ungrateful one."

Lee did not reply at once, although he took and retained the hand Falkner had impulsively extended. "Promise me," he said slowly, after a pause, "that you will say nothing yet to either of these women. I ask it for your own sake, and this girl's, not for mine. If, on the contrary, you are tempted to do so from any Quixotic idea of honor, remember that you will only precipitate something that will oblige you, from that same sense of honor, to separate from the girl forever."

"I don't understand."

"Enough!" said he, with a quick return of his old reckless gayety. "Shoot-Off-His-Mouth—the Beardless Boy Chief of the Sierras—has spoken! Let the Pale Face with the black moustache ponder and beware how he talks hereafter to the Rippling Cochituate Water! Go!"

Nevertheless, as soon as the door had closed upon Falkner, Lee's smile vanished. With his colorless face turned to the fading light at the window, the hollows in his temples and the lines in the corners of his eyes seemed to have grown more profound. He remained motionless and absorbed in thought so deep that the light rustle of a skirt, that would at other times have thrilled his sensitive ear, passed unheeded. At last, throwing off his reverie with the full and unrestrained sigh of a man who believes himself alone, he was startled by the soft laugh of Mrs. Hale, who had entered the room unperceived.

"Dear me! How portentous! Really, I almost feel as if I were interrupting a tete-a-tete between yourself and some old flame. I haven't heard anything so old-fashioned and conservative as that sigh since I have been in California. I thought you never had any Past out here?"

Fortunately his face was between her and the light, and the unmistakable expression of annoyance and impatience which was passed over it was spared her. There was, however, still enough dissonance in his manner to affect her quick feminine sense, and when she drew nearer to him it was with a certain maiden-like timidity.

"You are not worse, Mr. Lee, I hope? You have not over-exerted yourself?"

"There's little chance of that with one leg—if not in the grave at least mummified with bandages," he replied, with a bitterness new to him.

"Shall I loosen them? Perhaps they are too tight. There is nothing so irritating to one as the sensation of being tightly bound."

The light touch of her hand upon the rug that covered his knees, the thoughtful tenderness of the blue-veined lids, and the delicate atmosphere that seemed to surround her like a perfume cleared his face of its shadow and brought back the reckless fire into his blue eyes.

"I suppose I'm intolerant of all bonds," he said, looking at her intently, "in others as well as myself!"

Whether or not she detected any double meaning in his words, she was obliged to accept the challenge of his direct gaze, and, raising her eyes to his, drew back a little from him with a slight increase of color. "I was afraid you had heard bad news just now."

"What would you call bad news?" asked Lee, clasping his hands behind his head, and leaning back on the sofa, but without withdrawing his eyes from her face.

"Oh, any news that would interrupt your convalescence, or break up our little family party," said Mrs. Hale. "You have been getting on so well that really it would seem cruel to have anything interfere with our life of forgetting and being forgotten. But," she added with apprehensive quickness, "has anything happened? Is there really any news from—from, the trails? Yesterday Mr. Falkner said the snow had recommenced in the pass. Has he seen anything, noticed anything different?"

She looked so very pretty, with the rare, genuine, and youthful excitement that transfigured her wearied and wearying regularity of feature, that Lee contented himself with drinking in her prettiness as he would have inhaled the perfume of some flower.

"Why do you look at me so, Mr. Lee?" she asked, with a slight smile. "I believe something HAS happened. Mr. Falkner HAS brought you some intelligence."

"He has certainly found out something I did not foresee."

"And that troubles you?"

"It does."

"Is it a secret?"

"No."

"Then I suppose you will tell it to me at dinner," she said, with a little tone of relief.

"I am afraid, if I tell it at all, I must tell it now," he said, glancing at the door.

"You must do as you think best," she said coldly, "as it seems to be a secret, after all." She hesitated. "Kate is dressing, and will not be down for some time."

"So much the better. For I'm afraid that Ned has made a poor return to your hospitality by falling in love with her."

"Impossible! He has known her for scarcely a week."

"I am afraid we won't agree as to the length of time necessary to appreciate and love a woman. I think it can be done in seven days and four hours, the exact time we have been here."

"Yes; but as Kate was not in when you arrived, and did not come until later, you must take off at least one hour," said Mrs. Hale gayly.

"Ned can. I shall not abate a second."

"But are you not mistaken in his feelings?" she continued hurriedly. "He certainly has not said anything to her."

"That is his last hold on honor and reason. And to preserve that little intact he wants to run away at once."

"But that would be very silly."

"Do you think so?" he said, looking at her fixedly.

"Why not?" she asked in her turn, but rather faintly.

"I'll tell you why," he said, lowering his voice with a certain intensity of passion unlike his usual boyish lightheartedness. "Think of a man whose life has been one of alternate hardness and aggression, of savage disappointment and equally savage successes, who has known no other relaxation than dissipation and extravagance; a man to whom the idea of the domestic hearth and family ties only meant weakness, effeminacy, or—worse; who had looked for loyalty and devotion only in the man who battled for him at his right hand in danger, or shared his privations and sufferings. Think of such a man, and imagine that an accident has suddenly placed him in an atmosphere of purity, gentleness, and peace, surrounded him by the refinements of a higher life than he had ever known, and that he found himself as in a dream, on terms of equality with a pure woman who had never known any other life, and yet would understand and pity his. Imagine his loving her! Imagine that the first effect of that love was to show him his own inferiority and the immeasurable gulf that lay between his life and hers! Would he not fly rather than brave the disgrace of her awakening to the truth? Would he not fly rather than accept even the pity that might tempt her to a sacrifice?"

"But—is Mr. Falkner all that?"

"Nothing of the kind, I assure you!" said he demurely. "But that's the way a man in love feels."

"Really! Mr. Falkner should get you to plead his cause with Kate," said Mrs. Hale with a faint laugh.

"I need all my persuasive powers in that way for myself," said Lee boldly.

Mrs. Hale rose. "I think I hear Kate coming," she said. Nevertheless, she did not move away. "It IS Kate coming," she added hurriedly, stooping to pick up her work-basket, which had slipped with Lee's hand from her own.

It was Kate, who at once flew to her sister's assistance, Lee deploring from the sofa his own utter inability to aid her. "It's all my fault, too," he said to Kate, but looking at Mrs. Hale. "It seems I have a faculty of upsetting existing arrangements without the power of improving them, or even putting them back in their places. What shall I do? I am willing to hold any number of skeins or rewind any quantity of spools. I am even willing to forgive Ned for spending the whole day with you, and only bringing me the wing of a hawk for supper."

"That was all my folly, Mr. Lee," said Kate, with swift mendacity; "he was all the time looking after something for you, when I begged him to shoot a bird to get a feather for my hat. And that wing is SO pretty."

"It is a pity that mere beauty is not edible," said Lee, gravely, "and that if the worst comes to the worst here you would probably prefer me to Ned and his moustachios, merely because I've been tied by the leg to this sofa and slowly fattened like a Strasbourg goose."

Nevertheless, his badinage failed somehow to amuse Kate, and she presently excused herself to rejoin her sister, who had already slipped from the room. For the first time during their enforced seclusion a sense of restraint and uneasiness affected Mrs. Hale, her sister, and Falkner at dinner. The latter addressed himself to Mrs. Scott, almost entirely. Mrs. Hale was fain to bestow an exceptional and marked tenderness on her little daughter Minnie, who, however, by some occult childish instinct, insisted upon sharing it with Lee—her great friend—to Mrs. Hale's uneasy consciousness.

Nor was Lee slow to profit by the child's suggestion, but responded with certain vicarious caresses that increased the mother's embarrassment. That evening they retired early, but in the intervals of a restless night Kate was aware, from the sound of voices in the opposite room, that the friends were equally wakeful.

A morning of bright sunshine and soft warm air did not, however, bring any change to their new and constrained relations. It only seemed to offer a reason for Falkner to leave the house very early for his daily rounds, and gave Lee that occasion for unaided exercise with an extempore crutch on the veranda which allowed Mrs. Hale to pursue her manifold duties without the necessity of keeping him company. Kate also, as if to avoid an accidental meeting with Falkner, had remained at home with her sister. With one exception, they did not make their guests the subject of their usual playful comments, nor, after the fashion of their sex, quote their ideas and opinions. That exception was made by Mrs. Hale.

"You have had no difference with Mr. Falkner?" she said carelessly.

"No," said Kate quickly. "Why?"

"I only thought he seemed rather put out at dinner last night, and you didn't propose to go and meet him to-day."

"He must be bored with my company at times, I dare say," said Kate, with an indifference quite inconsistent with her rising color. "I shouldn't wonder if he was a little vexed with Mr. Lee's chaffing him about his sport yesterday, and probably intends to go further to-day, and bring home larger game. I think Mr. Lee very amusing always, but I sometimes fancy he lacks feeling."

"Feeling! You don't know him, Kate," said Mrs. Hale quickly. She stopped herself, but with a half-smiling recollection in her dropped eyelids.

"Well, he doesn't look very amiable now, stamping up and down the veranda. Perhaps you'd better go and soothe him."

"I'm really SO busy just now," said Mrs. Hale, with sudden and inconsequent energy; "things have got dreadfully behind in the last week. You had better go, Kate, and make him sit down, or he'll be overdoing it. These men never know any medium—in anything."

Contrary to Kate's expectation, Falkner returned earlier than usual, and, taking the invalid's arm, supported him in a more ambitious walk along the terrace before the house. They were apparently absorbed in conversation, but the two women who observed them from the window could not help noticing the almost feminine tenderness of Falkner's manner towards his wounded friend, and the thoughtful tenderness of his ministering care.

"I wonder," said Mrs. Hale, following them with softly appreciative eyes, "if women are capable of as disinterested friendship as men? I never saw anything like the devotion of these two creatures. Look! if Mr. Falkner hasn't got his arm round Mr. Lee's waist, and Lee, with his own arm over Falkner's neck, is looking up in his eyes. I declare, Kate, it almost seems an indiscretion to look at them."

Kate, however, to Mrs. Hale's indignation, threw her pretty head back and sniffed the air contemptuously. "I really don't see anything but some absurd sentimentalism of their own, or some mannish wickedness they're concocting by themselves. I am by no means certain, Josephine, that Lee's influence over that young man is the best thing for him."

"On the contrary! Lee's influence seems the only thing that checks his waywardness," said Mrs. Hale quickly. "I'm sure, if anyone makes sacrifices, it is Lee; I shouldn't wonder that even now he is making some concession to Falkner, and all those caressing ways of your friend are for a purpose. They're not much different from us, dear."

"Well, I wouldn't stand there and let them see me looking at them as if I couldn't bear them out of my sight for a moment," said Kate, whisking herself out of the room. "They're conceited enough, Heaven knows, already."

That evening, at dinner, however, the two men exhibited no trace of the restraint or uneasiness of the previous day. If they were less impulsive and exuberant, they were still frank and interested, and if the term could be used in connection with men apparently trained to neither self-control nor repose, there was a certain gentle dignity in their manner which for the time had the effect of lifting them a little above the social level of their entertainers. For even with all their predisposition to the strangers, Kate and Mrs. Hale had always retained a conscious attitude of gentle condescension and superiority towards them—an attitude not inconsistent with a stronger feeling, nor altogether unprovocative of it; yet this evening they found themselves impressed with something more than an equality in the men who had amused and interested them, and they were perhaps a little more critical and doubtful of their own power. Mrs. Hale's little girl, who had appreciated only the seriousness of the situation, had made her own application of it. "Are you dow'in' away from aunt Kate and mamma?" she asked, in an interval of silence.

"How else can I get you the red snow we saw at sunset, the other day, on the peak yonder?" said Lee gayly. "I'll have to get up some morning very early, and catch it when it comes at sunrise."

"What is this wonderful snow, Minnie, that you are tormenting Mr. Lee for?" asked Mrs. Hale.

"Oh! it's a fairy snow that he told me all about; it only comes when the sun comes up and goes down, and if you catch ever so little of it in your hand it makes all you fink you want come true! Wouldn't that be nice?" But to the child's astonishment her little circle of auditors, even while assenting, sighed.

The red snow was there plain enough the next morning before the valley was warm with light, and while Minnie, her mother, and aunt Kate were still peacefully sleeping. And Mr. Lee had kept his word, and was evidently seeking it, for he and Falkner were already urging their horses through the pass, with their faces towards and lit up by its glow.

Bret Harte

CHAPTER VIII

Kate was stirring early, but not as early as her sister, who met her on the threshold of her room. Her face was quite pale, and she held a letter in her hand. "What does this mean, Kate?"

"What is the matter?" asked Kate, her own color fading from her cheek.

"They are gone—with their horses. Left before day, and left this."

She handed Kate an open letter. The girl took it hurriedly, and read—

"When you get this we shall be no more; perhaps not even as much. Ned found the trail yesterday, and we are taking the first advantage of it before day. We dared not trust ourselves to say 'Good-by!' last evening; we were too cowardly to face you this morning; we must go as we came, without warning, but not without regret. We leave a package and a letter for your husband. It is not only our poor return for your gentleness and hospitality, but, since it was accidentally the means of giving us the pleasure of your society, we beg you to keep it in safety until his return. We kiss your mother's hands. Ned wants to say something more, but time presses, and I only allow him to send his love to Minnie, and to tell her that he is trying to find the red snow.

"GEORGE LEE."

"But he is not fit to travel," said Mrs. Hale. "And the trail—it may not be passable."

"It was passable the day before yesterday," said Kate drearily, "for I discovered it, and went as far as the buckeyes."

"Then it was you who told them about it," said Mrs. Hale reproachfully.

"No," said Kate indignantly. "Of course I didn't." She stopped, and, reading the significance of her speech in the glistening eyes of her sister, she blushed. Josephine kissed her, and said—

"It WAS treating us like children, Kate, but we must make them pay for it hereafter. For that package and letter to John means something, and we shall probably see them before long. I wonder what the letter is about, and what is in the package?"

"Probably one of Mr. Lee's jokes. He is quite capable of turning the whole thing into ridicule. I dare say he considers his visit here a prolonged jest."

"With his poor leg, Kate? You are as unfair to him as you were to Falkner when they first came."

Kate, however, kept her dark eyebrows knitted in a piquant frown.

Bret Harte

"To think of his intimating WHAT he would allow Falkner to say! And yet you believe he has no evil influence over the young man."

Mrs. Hale laughed. "Where are you going so fast, Kate?" she called mischievously, as the young lady flounced out of the room.

"Where? Why, to tidy John's room. He may be coming at any moment now. Or do you want to do it yourself?"

"No, no," returned Mrs. Hale hurriedly; "you do it. I'll look in a little later on."

She turned away with a sigh. The sun was shining brilliantly outside. Through the half-open blinds its long shafts seemed to be searching the house for the lost guests, and making the hollow shell appear doubly empty. What a contrast to the dear dark days of mysterious seclusion and delicious security, lit by Lee's laughter and the sparkling hearth, which had passed so quickly! The forgotten outer world seemed to have returned to the house through those open windows and awakened its dwellers from a dream.

The morning seemed interminable, and it was past noon, while they were deep in a sympathetic conference with Mrs. Scott, who had drawn a pathetic word-picture of the two friends perishing in the snow-drift, without flannels, brandy, smelling-salts, or jelly, which they had forgotten, when they were startled by the loud barking of "Spot" on the lawn before the house. The women looked hurriedly at each other.

"They have returned," said Mrs. Hale.

Kate ran to the window. A horseman was approaching the house. A single glance showed her that it was neither

Falkner, Lee, nor Hale, but a stranger.

"Perhaps he brings some news of them," said Mrs. Scott quickly. So complete had been their preoccupation with the loss of their guests that they could not yet conceive of anything that did not pertain to it.

The stranger, who was at once ushered into the parlor, was evidently disconcerted by the presence of the three women.

"I reckoned to see John Hale yer," he began, awkwardly.

A slight look of disappointment passed over their faces. "He has not yet returned," said Mrs. Hale briefly.

"Sho! I wanter know. He's hed time to do it, I reckon," said the stranger.

"I suppose he hasn't been able to get over from the Summit," returned Mrs. Hale. "The trail is closed."

"It ain't now, for I kem over it this mornin' myself."

"You didn't—meet—anyone?" asked Mrs. Hale timidly, with a glance at the others.

"No."

A long silence ensued. The unfortunate visitor plainly perceived an evident abatement of interest in himself, yet he still struggled politely to say something. "Then I reckon you know what kept Hale away?" he said dubiously.

"Oh, certainly—the stage robbery."

"I wish I'd known that," said the stranger reflectively, "for I ez good ez rode over jist to tell it to ye. Ye see John Hale, he sent a note to ye 'splainin' matters by a gentleman; but the road agents tackled that man, and left him for dead in the road."

"Yes," said Mrs. Hale impatiently.

"Luckily he didn't die, but kem to, and managed to crawl inter the brush, whar I found him when I was lookin' for stock, and brought him to my house—"

"YOU found him? YOUR house?" interrupted Mrs. Hale.

"Inter MY house," continued the man doggedly. "I'm Thompson of Thompson's Pass over yon; mebbe it ain't much of a house; but I brought him thar. Well, ez he couldn't find the note that Hale had guv him, and like ez not the road agents had gone through him and got it, ez soon ez the weather let up I made a break over yer to tell ye."

"You say Mr. Lee came to your house," repeated Mrs. Hale, "and is there now?"

"Not much," said the man grimly; "and I never said LEE was thar. I mean that Bilson waz shot by Lee and kem—"

"Certainly, Josephine!" said Kate, suddenly stepping between her sister and Thompson, and turning upon her a white face and eyes of silencing significance; "certainly—don't you remember?—that's the story we got from the Chinaman, you know, only muddled. Go on sir," she continued, turning to Thompson calmly; "you say that the man who brought the note from my brother was shot by Lee?"

"And another fellow they call Falkner. Yes, that's about the size of it."

"Thank you; it's nearly the same story that we heard. But you have had a long ride, Mr. Thompson; let me offer you a glass of whiskey in the dining-room. This way, please."

The door closed upon them none too soon. For Mrs. Hale already felt the room whirling around her, and sank back into her chair with a hysterical laugh. Old Mrs. Scott did not move from her seat, but, with her eyes fixed on the door, impatiently waited Kate's return. Neither spoke, but each felt that the young, untried girl was equal to the emergency, and would get at the truth.

The sound of Thompson's feet in the hall and the closing of the front door was followed by Kate's reappearance. Her face was still pale, but calm.

"Well?" said the two women in a breath.

"Well," returned Kate slowly; "Mr. Lee and Mr. Falkner were undoubtedly the two men who took the paper from John's messenger and brought it here."

"You are sure?" said Mrs. Scott.

"There can be no mistake, mother."

"THEN," said Mrs. Scott, with triumphant feminine logic, "I don't want anything more to satisfy me that they are PERFECTLY INNOCENT!"

More convincing than the most perfect masculine deduction, this single expression of their common nature sent a thrill of sympathy and understanding through each. They cried for a few moments on each other's shoulders. "To think," said Mrs. Scott, "what that poor boy must have suffered to have been obliged to do—that to—to—Bilson—isn't that the

Bret Harte

creature's name? I suppose we ought to send over there and inquire after him, with some chicken and jelly, Kate. It's only common humanity, and we must be just, my dear; for even if he shot Mr. Lee and provoked the poor boy to shoot him, he may have thought it his duty. And then, it will avert suspicions."

"To think," murmured Mrs. Hale, "what they must have gone through while they were here—momentarily expecting John to come, and yet keeping up such a light heart."

"I believe, if they had stayed any longer, they would have told us everything," said Mrs. Scott.

Both the younger women were silent. Kate was thinking of Falkner's significant speech as they neared the house on their last walk; Josephine was recalling the remorseful picture drawn by Lee, which she knew was his own portrait. Suddenly she started.

"But John will be here soon; what are we to tell him? And then that package and that letter."

"Don't be in a hurry to tell him anything at present, my child," said Mrs. Scott gently. "It is unfortunate this Mr. Thompson called here, but we are not obliged to understand what he says now about John's message, or to connect our visitors with his story. I'm sure, Kate, I should have treated them exactly as we did if they had come without any message from John; so I do not know why we should lay any stress on that, or even speak of it. The simple fact is that we have opened our house to two strangers in distress. Your husband," continued Mr. Hale's mother-in-law, "does not require to know more. As to the letter and package, we will keep that for further consideration. It cannot be of much importance, or they would have spoken of it before; it is probably some trifling present as a return for your hospitality. I should use no INDECOROUS haste in having it opened."

The two women kissed Mrs. Scott with a feeling of relief, and fell back into the monotony of their household duties. It is to be feared, however, that the absence of their outlawed guests was nearly as dangerous as their presence in the opportunity it afforded for uninterrupted and imaginative reflection. Both Kate and Josephine were at first shocked and wounded by the discovery of the real character of the two men with whom they had associated so familiarly, but it was no disparagement to their sense of propriety to say that the shock did not last long, and was accompanied with the fascination of danger. This was succeeded by a consciousness of the delicate flattery implied in their indirect influence over the men who had undoubtedly risked their lives for the sake of remaining with them. The best woman is not above being touched by the effect of her power over the worst man, and Kate at first allowed herself to think of Falkner in that light. But if in her later reflections he suffered as a heroic experience to be forgotten, he gained something as an actual man to be remembered. Now that the proposed rides from "his friend's house" were a part of the illusion, would he ever dare to visit them again? Would she dare to see him? She held her breath with a sudden pain of parting that was new to her; she tried to think of something else, to pick up the scattered threads of her life before that eventful day. But in vain; that one week had filled the place with implacable memories, or more terrible, as it seemed to her and her sister, they had both lost their feeble, alien hold upon Eagle's Court in the sudden presence of the real genii of these solitudes, and henceforth they alone would be the strangers there. They scarcely dared to confess it to each other, but this return to the dazzling sunlight and cloudless skies of the past appeared to them to be the one unreal experience; they had never known the true wild flavor of their home, except in that week of delicious isolation. Without breathing it aloud, they longed for some vague denoument to this experience that should take them from Eagle's Court forever.

It was noon the next day when the little household beheld the last shred of their illusion vanish like the melting snow in the strong sunlight of John Hale's return. He was accompanied by Colonel Clinch and Rawlins, two strangers to the women. Was it fancy, or the avenging spirit of their absent companions? but HE too looked a stranger, and as the little cavalcade wound its way up the slope he appeared to sit his horse and wear his hat with a certain slouch and absence of his usual restraint that strangely shocked them. Even the old half-condescending, half-punctilious gallantry of his greeting of his wife and family was changed, as he introduced his companions with a mingling of familiarity and shyness that was new to him. Did Mrs. Hale regret it, or feel a sense of relief in the absence of his usual seignorial formality? She only knew that she was grateful for the presence of the strangers, which for the moment postponed a matrimonial confidence from which she shrank.

"Proud to know you," said Colonel Clinch, with a sudden outbreak of the antique gallantry of some remote Huguenot ancestor. "My friend, Judge Hale, must be a regular Roman citizen to leave such a family and such a house at the call of public duty. Eh, Rawlins?"

"You bet," said Rawlins, looking from Kate to her sister in undisguised admiration.

"And I suppose the duty could not have been a very pleasant one," said Mrs. Hale, timidly, without looking at her husband.

"Gad, madam, that's just it," said the gallant Colonel, seating himself with a comfortable air, and an easy, though by no means disrespectful, familiarity. "We went into this fight a little more than a week ago. The only scrimmage we've had has been with the detectives that were on the robbers' track. Ha! ha! The best people we've met have been the friends of the men we were huntin', and we've generally come to the conclusion to vote the other ticket! Ez Judge Hale and me agreed ez we came along, the two men ez we'd most like to see just now and shake hands with are George Lee and Ned Falkner."

"The two leaders of the party who robbed the coach," explained Mr. Hale, with a slight return of his usual precision of statement.

The three women looked at each other with a blaze of thanksgiving in their grateful eyes. Without comprehending all that Colonel Clinch had said, they understood enough to know that their late guests were safe from the pursuit of that party, and that their own conduct was spared criticism. I hardly dare write it, but they instantly assumed the appearance of aggrieved martyrs, and felt as if they were!

"Yes, ladies!" continued the Colonel, inspired by the bright eyes fixed upon him. "We haven't taken the road ourselves yet, but—pohn honor—we wouldn't mind doing it in a case like this." Then with the fluent, but somewhat exaggerated, phraseology of a man trained to "stump" speaking, he gave an account of the robbery and his own connection with it. He spoke of the swindling and treachery which had undoubtedly provoked Falkner to obtain restitution of his property by an overt act of violence under the leadership of Lee. He added that he had learned since at Wild Cat Station that Harkins had fled the country, that a suit had been commenced by the Excelsior Ditch Company, and that all available property of

Harkins had been seized by the sheriff.

"Of course it can't be proved yet, but there's no doubt in my mind that Lee, who is an old friend of Ned Falkner's, got up that job to help him, and that Ned's off with the money by this time—and I'm right glad of it. I can't say ez we've done much towards it, except to keep tumbling in the way of that detective party of Stanner's, and so throw them off the trail— ha, ha! The Judge here, I reckon, has had his share of fun, for while he was at Hennicker's trying to get some facts from Hennicker's pretty daughter, Stanner tried to get up some sort of vigilance committee of the stage passengers to burn down Hennicker's ranch out of spite, but the Judge here stepped in and stopped that."

"It was really a high-handed proceeding, Josephine, but I managed to check it," said Hale, meeting somewhat consciously the first direct look his wife had cast upon him, and falling back for support on his old manner. "In its way, I think it was worse than the robbery by Lee and Falkner, for it was done in the name of law and order; while, as far as I can judge from the facts, the affair that we were following up was simply a rude and irregular restitution of property that had been morally stolen."

"I have no doubt you did quite right, though I don't under-stand it," said Mrs. Hale languidly; "but I trust these gentlemen will stay to luncheon, and in the meantime excuse us for running away, as we are short of servants, and Manuel seems to have followed the example of the head of the house and left us, in pursuit of somebody or something."

When the three women had gained the vantage-ground of the drawing-room, Kate said, earnestly, "As it's all right, hadn't we better tell him now?"

"Decidedly not, child," said Mrs. Scott, imperatively. "Do you suppose they are in a hurry to tell us THEIR whole story? Who are those Hennicker people? and they were there a week ago!"

"And did you notice John's hat when he came in, and the vulgar familiarity of calling him 'Judge'?" said Mrs. Hale.

"Well, certainly anything like the familiarity of this man Clinch I never saw," said Kate. "Contrast his manner with Mr. Falkner's."

At luncheon the three suffering martyrs finally succeeded in reducing Hale and his two friends to an attitude of vague apology. But their triumph was short-lived. At the end of the meal they were startled by the trampling of hoofs without, followed by loud knocking. In another moment the door was opened, and Mr. Stanner strode into the room. Hale rose with a look of indignation.

"I thought, as Mr. Stanner understood that I had no desire for his company elsewhere, he would hardly venture to intrude upon me in my house, and certainly not after—"

"Ef you're alluding to the Vigilantes shakin' you and Zeenie up at Hennicker's, you can't make ME responsible for that. I'm here now on business—you understand—reg'lar business. Ef you want to see the papers yer ken. I suppose you know what a warrant is?"

"I know what YOU are," said Hale hotly; "and if you don't leave my house—"

"Steady, boys," interrupted Stanner, as his five henchmen filed into the hall. "There's no backin' down here, Colonel Clinch, unless you and Hale kalkilate to back down the State of Californy! The matter stands like this. There's a half-breed Mexican, called Manuel, arrested over at the Summit, who swears he saw George Lee and Edward Falkner in this house the night after the robbery. He says that they were makin' themselves at home here, as if they were among friends, and considerin' the kind of help we've had from Mr. John Hale, it looks ez if it might be true."

"It's an infamous lie!" said Hale.

"It may be true, John," said Mrs. Scott, suddenly stepping in front of her pale-cheeked daughters. "A wounded man was brought here out of the storm by his friend, who claimed the shelter of your roof. As your mother I should have been unworthy to stay beneath it and have denied that shelter or withheld it until I knew his name and what he was. He stayed here until he could be removed. He left a letter for you. It will probably tell you if he was the man this person is seeking."

"Thank you, mother," said Hale, lifting her hand to his lips quietly; "and perhaps you will kindly tell these gentlemen that, as your son does not care to know who or what the stranger was, there is no necessity for opening the letter, or keeping Mr. Stanner a moment longer."

"But you will oblige ME, John, by opening it before these gentlemen," said Mrs. Hale recovering her voice and color. "Please to follow me," she said preceding them to the staircase.

They entered Mr. Hale's room, now restored to its original condition. On the table lay a letter and a small package. The eyes of Mr. Stanner, a little abashed by the attitude of the two women, fastened upon it and glistened.

Josephine handed her husband the letter. He opened it in breathless silence and read—

"JOHN HALE,

"We owe you no return for voluntarily making yourself a champion of justice and pursuing us, except it was to offer you a fair field and no favor. We didn't get that much from you, but accident brought us into your house and into your family, where we DID get it, and were fairly vanquished. To the victors belong the spoils. We leave the package of greenbacks which we took from Colonel Clinch in the Sierra coach, but which was first stolen by Harkins from forty-four shareholders of the Excelsior Ditch. We have no right to say what YOU should do with it, but if you aren't tired of following the same line of justice that induced you to run after US, you will try to restore it to its rightful owners.

"We leave you another trifle as an evidence that our intrusion into your affairs was not without some service to you, even if the service was as accidental as the intrusion. You will find a pair of boots in the corner of your closet. They were taken from the burglarious feet of Manuel, your peon, who, believing the three ladies were alone and at his mercy, entered your house with an accomplice at two o'clock on the morning of the 21st, and was kicked out by

"Your obedient servants,

"GEORGE LEE & EDWARD FALKNER"

Hale's voice and color changed on reading this last paragraph. He turned quickly towards his wife; Kate flew to the closet, where the muffled boots of Manuel confronted them.

"We never knew it. I always suspected something that night," said Mrs. Hale and Mrs. Scott in the same breath.

"That's all very well, and like George Lee's high falutin'," said Stanner, approaching the table, "but as long ez the greenbacks are here he can make what capital he likes outer Manuel. I'll trouble you to pass over that package."

"Excuse me," said Hale, "but I believe this is the package taken from Colonel Clinch. Is it not?" he added, appealing to the Colonel.

"It is," said Clinch.

"Then take it," said Hale, handing him the package. "The first restitution is to you, but I believe you will fulfil Lee's instructions as well as myself."

"But," said Stanner, furiously interposing, "I've a warrant to seize that wherever found, and I dare you to disobey the law."

"Mr. Stanner," said Clinch, slowly, "there are ladies present. If you insist upon having that package I must ask them to withdraw, and I'm afraid you'll find me better prepared to resist a SECOND robbery than I was the first. Your warrant, which was taken out by the Express Company, is supplanted by civil proceedings taken the day before yesterday against the property of the fugitive swindler Harkins! You should have consulted the sheriff before you came here."

Stanner saw his mistake. But in the faces of his grinning followers he was obliged to keep up his bluster. "You shall hear from me again, sir," he said, turning on his heel.

"I beg your pardon," said Clinch grimly, "but do I understand that at last I am to have the honor—"

"You shall hear from the Company's lawyers, sir," said Stanner turning red, and noisily leaving the room.

"And so, my dear ladies," said Colonel Clinch, "you have spent a week with a highwayman. I say A highwayman, for it would be hard to call my young friend Falkner by that name for his first offence, committed under great provocation, and undoubtedly instigated by Lee, who was an old friend of his, and to whom he came, no doubt, in desperation."

Kate stole a triumphant glance at her sister, who dropped her lids over her glistening eyes. "And this Mr. Lee," she continued more gently, "is he really a highwayman?"

"George Lee," said Clinch, settling himself back oratorically in his chair, "my dear young lady, IS a highwayman, but not of the common sort. He is a gentleman born, madam, comes from one of the oldest families of the Eastern Shore of Maryland. He never mixes himself up with anything but some of the biggest strikes, and he's an educated man. He is very popular with ladies and children; he was never known to do or say anything that could bring a blush to the cheek of beauty or a tear to the eye of innocence. I think I may say I'm sure you found him so."

"I shall never believe him anything but a gentleman," said Mrs. Scott, firmly.

"If he has a defect, it is perhaps a too reckless indulgence in draw poker," said the Colonel, musingly; "not unbecoming a gentleman, understand me, Mrs. Scott, but perhaps too reckless for his own good. George played a grand game, a glittering game, but pardon me if I say an UNCERTAIN game. I've told him so; it's the only point on which we ever differed."

"Then you know him?" said Mrs. Hale, lifting her soft eyes to the Colonel.

"I have that honor."

"Did his appearance, Josephine," broke in Hale, somewhat ostentatiously, "appear to—er—er—correspond with these qualities? You know what I mean."

"He certainly seemed very simple and natural," said Mrs. Hale, slightly drawing her pretty lips together. "He did not wear his trousers rolled up over his boots in the company of ladies, as you're doing now, nor did he make his first appearance in this house with such a hat as you wore this morning, or I should not have admitted him."

There were a few moments of embarrassing silence.

"Do you intend to give that package to Mr. Falkner yourself, Colonel?" asked Mrs. Scott.

"I shall hand it over to the Excelsior Company," said the Colonel, "but I shall inform Ned of what I have done."

"Then," said Mrs. Scott, "will you kindly take a message from us to him?"

"If you wish it."

"You will be doing ME a great favor, Colonel," said Hale, politely.

 Whatever the message was, six months later it brought Edward Falkner, the reestablished superintendent of the

Excelsior Ditch, to Eagle's Court. As he and Kate stood again on the plateau, looking towards the distant slopes once more green with verdure, Falkner said—

"Everything here looks as it did the first day I saw it, except your sister."

"The place does not agree with her," said Kate hurriedly. "That is why my brother thinks of leaving it before the winter sets in."

"It seems so sad," said Falkner, "for the last words poor George said to me, as he left to join his cousin's corps at Richmond, were: 'If I'm not killed, Ned, I hope some day to stand again beside Mrs. Hale, at the window in Eagle's Court, and watch you and Kate coming home!'"

ABOUT THE AUTHOR

 **Francis Bret Harte** (August 25, 1836–May 6, 1902) was an American author and poet, best remembered for his accounts of pioneering life in California.

Born in Albany, New York, Harte moved to California in 1853, later working there in a number of capacities, including miner, teacher, messenger, and journalist. He spent part of his life in the northern California coast town now known as Arcata, at the time it was just a mining camp on Humboldt Bay.

His first literary efforts, including poetry and prose, appeared in The Californian, an early literary journal edited by Charles Henry Webb. In 1868 he became editor of The Overland Monthly, another new literary magazine, but this one more in tune with the pioneering spirit of excitement in California. His story, "The Luck of Roaring Camp," appeared in the magazine's second edition, propelling Harte to nationwide fame.

As an established literary figure, he was appointed to the position of United States Consul in the town of Krefeld, Germany in 1878 and Glasgow in 1880. In 1885 he settled in London. During the thirty years he spent in Europe, he never abandoned writing, and maintained a prodigious output of stories that retained the freshness of his earlier work. He died in England in 1902.

Choose from Thousands of 1stWorldLibrary Classics By

A. M. Barnard
Ada Leverson
Adolphus William Ward
Aesop
Agatha Christie
Alexander Aaronsohn
Alexander Kielland
Alexandre Dumas
Alfred Gatty
Alfred Ollivant
Alice Duer Miller
Alice Turner Curtis
Alice Dunbar
Allen Chapman
Alleyne Ireland
Ambrose Bierce
Amelia E. Barr
Amory H. Bradford
Andrew Lang
Andrew McFarland Davis
Andy Adams
Angela Brazil
Anna Alice Chapin
Anna Sewell
Annie Besant
Annie Hamilton Donnell
Annie Payson Call
Annie Roe Carr
Annonaymous
Anton Chekhov
Archibald Lee Fletcher
Arnold Bennett
Arthur C. Benson
Arthur Conan Doyle
Arthur M. Winfield
Arthur Ransome
Arthur Schnitzler
Arthur Train
Atticus
B.H. Baden-Powell
B. M. Bower
B. C. Chatterjee
Baroness Emmuska Orczy
Baroness Orczy
Basil King
Bayard Taylor
Ben Macomber
Bertha Muzzy Bower
Bjornstjerne Bjornson

Booth Tarkington
Boyd Cable
Bram Stoker
C. Collodi
C. E. Orr
C. M. Ingleby
Carolyn Wells
Catherine Parr Traill
Charles A. Eastman
Charles Amory Beach
Charles Dickens
Charles Dudley Warner
Charles Farrar Browne
Charles Ives
Charles Kingsley
Charles Klein
Charles Hanson Towne
Charles Lathrop Pack
Charles Romyn Dake
Charles Whibley
Charles Willing Beale
Charlotte M. Braeme
Charlotte M. Yonge
Charlotte Perkins Stetson
Clair W. Hayes
Clarence Day Jr.
Clarence E. Mulford
Clemence Housman
Confucius
Coningsby Dawson
Cornelis DeWitt Wilcox
Cyril Burleigh
D. H. Lawrence
Daniel Defoe
David Garnett
Dinah Craik
Don Carlos Janes
Donald Keyhoe
Dorothy Kilner
Dougan Clark
Douglas Fairbanks
E. Nesbit
E. P. Roe
E. Phillips Oppenheim
E. S. Brooks
Earl Barnes
Edgar Rice Burroughs
Edith Van Dyne
Edith Wharton

Edward Everett Hale
Edward J. O'Biren
Edward S. Ellis
Edwin L. Arnold
Eleanor Atkins
Eleanor Hallowell Abbott
Eliot Gregory
Elizabeth Gaskell
Elizabeth McCracken
Elizabeth Von Arnim
Ellem Key
Emerson Hough
Emilie F. Carlen
Emily Bronte
Emily Dickinson
Enid Bagnold
Enilor Macartney Lane
Erasmus W. Jones
Ernie Howard Pie
Ethel May Dell
Ethel Turner
Ethel Watts Mumford
Eugene Sue
Eugenie Foa
Eugene Wood
Eustace Hale Ball
Evelyn Everett-green
Everard Cotes
F. H. Cheley
F. J. Cross
F. Marion Crawford
Fannie E. Newberry
Federick Austin Ogg
Ferdinand Ossendowski
Fergus Hume
Florence A. Kilpatrick
Fremont B. Deering
Francis Bacon
Francis Darwin
Frances Hodgson Burnett
Frances Parkinson Keyes
Frank Gee Patchin
Frank Harris
Frank Jewett Mather
Frank L. Packard
Frank V. Webster
Frederic Stewart Isham
Frederick Trevor Hill
Frederick Winslow Taylor

Friedrich Kerst
Friedrich Nietzsche
Fyodor Dostoyevsky
G.A. Henty
G.K. Chesterton
Gabrielle E. Jackson
Garrett P. Serviss
Gaston Leroux
George A. Warren
George Ade
Geroge Bernard Shaw
George Cary Eggleston
George Durston
George Ebers
George Eliot
George Gissing
George MacDonald
George Meredith
George Orwell
George Sylvester Viereck
George Tucker
George W. Cable
George Wharton James
Gertrude Atherton
Gordon Casserly
Grace E. King
Grace Gallatin
Grace Greenwood
Grant Allen
Guillermo A. Sherwell
Gulielma Zollinger
Gustav Flaubert
H. A. Cody
H. B. Irving
H.C. Bailey
H. G. Wells
H. H. Munro
H. Irving Hancock
H. R. Naylor
H. Rider Haggard
H. W. C. Davis
Haldeman Julius
Hall Caine
Hamilton Wright Mabie
Hans Christian Andersen
Harold Avery
Harold McGrath
Harriet Beecher Stowe
Harry Castlemon
Harry Coghill
Harry Houidini

Hayden Carruth
Helent Hunt Jackson
Helen Nicolay
Hendrik Conscience
Hendy David Thoreau
Henri Barbusse
Henrik Ibsen
Henry Adams
Henry Ford
Henry Frost
Henry James
Henry Jones Ford
Henry Seton Merriman
Henry W Longfellow
Herbert A. Giles
Herbert Carter
Herbert N. Casson
Herman Hesse
Hildegard G. Frey
Homer
Honore De Balzac
Horace B. Day
Horace Walpole
Horatio Alger Jr.
Howard Pyle
Howard R. Garis
Hugh Lofting
Hugh Walpole
Humphry Ward
Ian Maclaren
Inez Haynes Gillmore
Irving Bacheller
Isabel Cecilia Williams
Isabel Hornibrook
Israel Abrahams
Ivan Turgenev
J.G.Austin
J. Henri Fabre
J. M. Barrie
J. M. Walsh
J. Macdonald Oxley
J. R. Miller
J. S. Fletcher
J. S. Knowles
J. Storer Clouston
J. W. Duffield
Jack London
Jacob Abbott
James Allen
James Andrews
James Baldwin

James Branch Cabell
James DeMille
James Joyce
James Lane Allen
James Lane Allen
James Oliver Curwood
James Oppenheim
James Otis
James R. Driscoll
Jane Abbott
Jane Austen
Jane L. Stewart
Janet Aldridge
Jens Peter Jacobsen
Jerome K. Jerome
Jessie Graham Flower
John Buchan
John Burroughs
John Cournos
John F. Kennedy
John Gay
John Glasworthy
John Habberton
John Joy Bell
John Kendrick Bangs
John Milton
John Philip Sousa
John Taintor Foote
Jonas Lauritz Idemil Lie
Jonathan Swift
Joseph A. Altsheler
Joseph Carey
Joseph Conrad
Joseph E. Badger Jr
Joseph Hergesheimer
Joseph Jacobs
Jules Vernes
Julian Hawthrone
Julie A Lippmann
Justin Huntly McCarthy
Kakuzo Okakura
Karle Wilson Baker
Kate Chopin
Kenneth Grahame
Kenneth McGaffey
Kate Langley Bosher
Kate Langley Bosher
Katherine Cecil Thurston
Katherine Stokes
L. A. Abbot
L. T. Meade

L. Frank Baum
Latta Griswold
Laura Dent Crane
Laura Lee Hope
Laurence Housman
Lawrence Beasley
Leo Tolstoy
Leonid Andreyev
Lewis Carroll
Lewis Sperry Chafer
Lilian Bell
Lloyd Osbourne
Louis Hughes
Louis Joseph Vance
Louis Tracy
Louisa May Alcott
Lucy Fitch Perkins
Lucy Maud Montgomery
Luther Benson
Lydia Miller Middleton
Lyndon Orr
M. Corvus
M. H. Adams
Margaret E. Sangster
Margret Howth
Margaret Vandercook
Margaret W. Hungerford
Margret Penrose
Maria Edgeworth
Maria Thompson Daviess
Mariano Azuela
Marion Polk Angellotti
Mark Overton
Mark Twain
Mary Austin
Mary Catherine Crowley
Mary Cole
Mary Hastings Bradley
Mary Roberts Rinehart
Mary Rowlandson
M. Wollstonecraft Shelley
Maud Lindsay
Max Beerbohm
Myra Kelly
Nathaniel Hawthrone
Nicolo Machiavelli
O. F. Walton
Oscar Wilde

Owen Johnson
P.G. Wodehouse
Paul and Mabel Thorne
Paul G. Tomlinson
Paul Severing
Percy Brebner
Percy Keese Fitzhugh
Peter B. Kyne
Plato
Quincy Allen
R. Derby Holmes
R. L. Stevenson
R. S. Ball
Rabindranath Tagore
Rahul Alvares
Ralph Bonehill
Ralph Henry Barbour
Ralph Victor
Ralph Waldo Emmerson
Rene Descartes
Ray Cummings
Rex Beach
Rex E. Beach
Richard Harding Davis
Richard Jefferies
Richard Le Gallienne
Robert Barr
Robert Frost
Robert Gordon Anderson
Robert L. Drake
Robert Lansing
Robert Lynd
Robert Michael Ballantyne
Robert W. Chambers
Rosa Nouchette Carey
Rudyard Kipling
Saint Augustine
Samuel B. Allison
Samuel Hopkins Adams
Sarah Bernhardt
Sarah C. Hallowell
Selma Lagerlof
Sherwood Anderson
Sigmund Freud
Standish O'Grady
Stanley Weyman
Stella Benson
Stella M. Francis

Stephen Crane
Stewart Edward White
Stijn Streuvels
Swami Abhedananda
Swami Parmananda
T. S. Ackland
T. S. Arthur
The Princess Der Ling
Thomas A. Janvier
Thomas A Kempis
Thomas Anderton
Thomas Bailey Aldrich
Thomas Bulfinch
Thomas De Quincey
Thomas Dixon
Thomas H. Huxley
Thomas Hardy
Thomas More
Thornton W. Burgess
U. S. Grant
Upton Sinclair
Valentine Williams
Various Authors
Vaughan Kester
Victor Appleton
Victor G. Durham
Victoria Cross
Virginia Woolf
Wadsworth Camp
Walter Camp
Walter Scott
Washington Irving
Wilbur Lawton
Wilkie Collins
Willa Cather
Willard F. Baker
William Dean Howells
William le Queux
W. Makepeace Thackeray
William W. Walter
William Shakespeare
Winston Churchill
Yei Theodora Ozaki
Yogi Ramacharaka
Young E. Allison
Zane Grey